Andy & Sofía

ISBN 978-0615422374

Website: www.andy.org.mx

Blog: blog.andy.org.mx

Videos: www.youtube.com/a3vino

Pictures: www.flickr.com/photos/a3vino

Social media: Facebook: /onefitsavior

Twitter: @atrevino

Andy & Sofía

stem cells, scientific miracles

and

"one fit savior"

by

Andrés Treviño

with

Kate Kruschwitz

To:

My children, Andy, Sofía and Tania

And my wife, Ana Paulina

Author's Acknowledgement

I'd like to express my thanks to Kate Kruschwitz, without whom our story never would have become this book. She spent countless weekends, outside of her job as a writer at Children's Hospital Boston, shaping my detailed journal entries into a coherent literary narrative. I'm deeply grateful for her skill, sensitivity, generosity and instinct. And her friendship.

Andrés Treviño
May, 2011

Table of Contents

PROLOGUE

Stem Cell Dad

In September, 2008, I paid a visit to Paul Lerou, MD, PhD, at the Stem Cell Program at Children's Hospital Boston. He greeted me at the door of his lab—the same youthful, bespectacled guy I'd met several years ago, his slender frame clad in khakis and a plaid shirt. The last time I'd seen him, he was wearing scrubs and a lab coat, part of a team of Children's doctors treating my critically ill son. Now he was running his own laboratory within the stem cell program, investigating blood and immune disorders. He's both a physician and a scientist.

On this September afternoon, he invited me into a small, equipment-laden room, where he removed a tiny glass dish from an incubator. He positioned the dish under a microscope, adjusted the lens and stepped back. "OK, Andrés, have a look."

In the microscope's radiant field, I saw pale spherical clouds spread on a sparkling background. These living clouds contained thousands of embryonic stem cells, known as ESCs, grown from a cluster of just a couple of hundred cells making up a human embryo. Gathered on a dense galaxy of nurturing feeder cells, the ESCs seemed to glow with an almost magical beauty.

These embryonic cells are infinitesimally small yet infinitely creative, capable of endlessly replicating themselves, becoming any organ or tissue in the body. They are pluripotent powerhouses, following DNA-coded pathways to become blood or bone, liver or lung, egg or sperm. Once an embryo is fully formed into a fetus, some of the cells, called adult stem cells, retain the ability to replicate—generating among other things, the new blood cells that sustain life. Harnessing their unique power holds enormous potential for disease treatment. We already know how a blood stem cell transplant (also called bone marrow transplant) can replace a blood system destroyed by disease. Scientists like Paul Lerou are now finding ways to direct stem cells to become healthy replacements for other defective cells, such as cardiac muscle cells damaged by a heart attack or neurons destroyed by a spinal cord injury. I realized I was looking at the future of medicine.

I raised my head from the scope, feeling a combination of awe and excitement mixed with a deeper emotion. Each cell I was viewing carried a genetic blueprint that was half mine. I was the father of those embryonic stem cells.

I turned to Lerou. "This is very cool."

Lerou smiled and said, "Well, you're looking at a brand-new stem cell line we've created from an embryo you and your wife donated. It's an amazing addition to our research here."

The significance of stem cell research is not theoretical to me and my wife, Paulina. Our son, Andy, was born with an inherited immune disease—his blood cells couldn't defend him against infection. His small body was continually ravaged by viruses, bacteria and other bugs a healthy person could easily fight. Doctors at Children's Hospital told us Andy's only hope was a blood stem cell transplant to replace his immune system. But the transplanted cells had to come from a donor whose genetic type matched our son's, or his body would reject them. A special blood test could analyze a particular series of molecules in a donor's white blood cells, looking for very specific compatibilities with Andy's. Without those compatibilities, the transplant would fail.

We searched donor registries worldwide, to no avail—there were no matches. We were told we'd have to rely on a long shot, using *in vitro* fertilization to try to create a "test tube baby" sibling whose blood profile was the same as our son's. After birth, this baby's umbilical cord blood, rich in stem cells, would provide the transplant. More than just finding a match, we needed to make sure this child didn't also have Andy's deadly disease. The odds weren't great.

While medications with dangerous side effects kept our little boy alive, we waited two years for the invention of a unique genetic test for the inherited disorder. We endured a grueling 24 months of hormone shots, egg harvests, sperm collections and many attempts to coax eggs and sperm to mix successfully in a petri dish. Finally, fertility doctors were able to produce a matched embryo who also tested free of the disease—an embryo with the right stuff. They implanted the embryo in my wife. By the time our beautiful daughter, Sofía, was born, we knew she was the most miraculous baby in the world.

IVF embryos with a genetic disease can't be implanted and are usually destroyed as medical waste. But Paulina and I knew our leftover embryos would be valuable for research. Their genes held secrets that could contribute to understanding Andy's immune deficiency, as well as other immune and blood diseases affecting millions of people. Studying these cells could lead to life-saving breakthroughs. We eagerly donated the frozen embryos remaining from our search for Sofía to one of the premier stem cell research programs in the world, at Children's Hospital Boston.

However, we were disappointed to learn those thawed embryos weren't robust enough for research. They were discarded.

Years later, when Paulina and I decided to have a third child and knew we'd have to go through *IVF* again, we hoped this time our unusable leftover embryos would be more viable. As it happened, they were. We gave them to Children's, hoping that someday, somewhere, a child born with an immune disease like Andy's won't have to suffer as he did.

PART ONE

EXTREME PARENTHOOD

Chapter One
Life, and an Ordeal, Begin

May 15, 1999, 7:19 p.m. *"¡Un niño!"* the obstetrician pronounced, holding up my newborn son like a prize-winning fish. When Andy announced himself with a wail I felt as though I had a new set of ears.

"I believe you wanted to cut the umbilicus?" the doctor asked politely, handing me a pair of tiny scissors. "It's a beautiful, healthy cord." My hands shook slightly—the cord was so thick it took several snips. I watched as the pediatrician, Dr. Irene Maulen, weighed, measured and pronounced Andy a solid "9" on the Apgar test. Then she placed the swaddled baby on my wife's chest. Paulina's face glowed. Just a few hours ago, waiting for the anesthesiologist, she'd bitten my arm. Now all that pain and pushing seemed forgotten.

My older sister, Veronica, a Lamaze birthing coach, was in the delivery room, and she snapped the first photo of us as a new family. In it, Paulina seems much younger than her 26 years— she looks like a pretty brunette teenager without a speck of makeup. I still had some hair at 28, but I was losing it fast. At a solidly built 6' 3", I tower over her and make her look even more petite. Andy appears as a blanketed bump in Paulina's arms.

We immediately unwrapped Andy like a present, kissing his hands and feet.

"Look, Andrés, how tiny!" Paulina whispered, her voice husky.

"He's perfect," I answered. His heartbeat fluttered under my fingertips and I suddenly felt giddy. What astonishing beauty we had made. Andy looked at us with big, dark eyes as if he recognized us, and turned his face to Paulina's breast.

She laughed softly, "He already knows exactly what to do."

Outside the delivery room, our parents, siblings and other assorted relatives overflowed the lounge into the hallway, waiting to congratulate us and glimpse the newest family member as he was whisked to the nursery.

We were ensconced at the brand-new Hospital Angeles de las Lomas in

Huixquilucan on the outskirts of Mexico City. Mexican public healthcare is a disaster, and anyone who can afford health insurance uses privately-owned hospitals like this one. Hospital Angeles felt like a five-star hotel, and everything had that just-out-of-the-box look, even the nurses. Our private room was luxurious—pale yellow walls with matching bed linens, cable TV and a sleep sofa for me. I was happy to have a little pampering while we absorbed the stunning reality that we'd become parents.

After our families finally left, I pushed the sofa against my wife's bed so we could hold hands before falling into exhausted sleep. "I can't believe he's finally here," she murmured drowsily. "So perfect…"

Before dawn I awakened from a familiar, happy dream—I was 11 or 12, roaming the forest on my grandfather's coffee farm with my cousin, Mauricio, following little streams and looking for waterfalls. The dream faded, but as I thought of my son, it felt like Christmas morning.

Heat

When Paulina woke I helped her walk down the hall to the nursery, where five babies were displayed like exotic fruit behind plate glass. In the closet-sized lactation room, a nurse handed me my son, cocooned in blankets and a yellow knit cap. I held the sweet, solid weight of my first-born, tucked against my chest. I bent my face to kiss him. His cheek felt scalding.

"He seems awfully warm," I said.

"Much too hot! Take off this blanket," Paulina commanded.

The nurse was dismissive. "Oh, it's nothing, we put him under a lamp because he looked a little jaundiced," she replied. But Andy started to cry, and wouldn't take the nipple. The nurse and Paulina tried every position except upside down, while Andy kept squalling, rigid with distress. Finally, the nurse wrapped him up and took him back to his crib, saying she'd check the baby's temperature and notify our pediatrician. Paulina used the breast pump and I helped her back to bed, both of us feeling at a loss.

Later, Dr. Maulen appeared in our room, her brow furrowed. She was a fashionably-dressed woman in her 40s, with bright lipstick and a direct manner. I didn't like her much; she seemed too aggressively stylish to be a serious doctor.

"Your baby has a fever and that's never a good sign," she said. "We're trying to bring his temperature down."

I grabbed Paulina's hand.

"We'll do a blood test to see if he has an infection, in which case he'll need intravenous antibiotics. In the meantime, we'll have to move him out of the nursery into the MCU—the Medium Care Unit. He's a risk to the other babies if he has something contagious."

"What—how did this happen? What does this mean?" I stammered.

"That's unclear. I've asked one of my colleagues, a neonatologist, to give us a second opinion. He's off duty today, but he'll stop by in a few hours, and we'll talk then. I'm sorry." She left the room.

My heart was pounding and I wasn't sure what to do with a sickening surge of fear and anger. Serious illness was unprecedented in my immediate family. I've never liked visiting hospitals; I hated the way they smelled. But so far, neither my parents nor my brother and sister had ever been sick enough to be hospitalized. Veronica had gone home with each of her two babies a day after the birth, and we'd expected the same uncomplicated scenario. I restrained an urge to punch the pastel walls in anxiety. Paulina turned to me tearfully, so I held her until we both calmed down. Then we called our parents. My father, Victor, my mother, Marilu, and Paulina's folks, Alfredo and Lupita, had been waiting for visiting hours. My mother's a rock-steady woman, and I didn't like hearing the worry in her voice as she said, "We'll be right over."

After they arrived I went to check on Andy in the MCU. He was asleep on his back in a clear plastic incubator, arms raised, fists flanking his head. I drew up a chair to study my son, marveling at his impossibly miniature fingernails, his tiny nostrils and spiky eyelashes. I listened to his soft breathing and longed to hear a lusty cry—anything to show he was a strong, healthy baby.

Soon, a young doctor in green scrubs asked me if I wanted to accompany Andy while his blood was drawn. The treatment room next to the MCU looked and smelled like my high school chemistry lab. The baby-faced doctor looked like a high school student, too—a nervous one. He examined the back of Andy's hand, about the size of a postage stamp, under a lamp, pinching hard, searching for a vein. Then he picked up a 3-inch needle. Andy started wailing. Suddenly I broke into a sweat and the room swayed—the doctor glanced at me and said, "Better lie on the floor and elevate your feet." From my prone position, I saw Andy's blood being drawn and he was hooked up to an intravenous drip. The sight of the IV implanted in such tender flesh made my stomach twist. Then I got to my feet in shame. *Get a grip!* Is this what fatherhood was about? I've always hated needles, but I couldn't start fainting at them now.

It was close to midnight when Dr. Garcia, the consulting neonatologist, arrived in our room. He was tall, with slicked-back hair, dressed in khaki slacks, a polo shirt and tennis shoes. "I've examined the baby and I'm not too concerned¬," he said, casually. "I think the fever was caused by a low sodium level, a stress reaction to the long labor. He's not feverish now and I think he'll be even better in the morning. The blood test will probably show nothing, but the antibiotics will be a good precaution, just in case."

I glanced at Dr. Maulen for reassurance, but she pursed her painted lips and looked unconvinced. "That's good news, isn't it?" I asked. She didn't reply. Then both doctors said good night and left.

My mother hugged us, her face bright with relief. "Don't forget to use the CD player you brought—he should have music while he's in the MCU," she said.

My dad squeezed my shoulder, "We'll explain to the rest of the family. Get some sleep."

Finally alone with Paulina, I opened the convertible couch as she settled back in her hospital bed, where she looked like a worried, rumpled child.

"So, it was just a little stress reaction," she said. "Not such a big deal. Andy will be fine, right? I just wish I could hold him."

"I know. Me too."

I told her about my fainting spell, to make her smile. And she did.

"You're just a big baby about needles."

When I turned off the light, she said again, "He *will* be OK, right?"

"He'll be OK," I answered. Mercifully, I fell asleep before I could complete another thought.

Going nowhere

A week later, Andy was still in the MCU, serving out the 10-day course of intravenous antibiotics. Outside the hospital, the world of work and weather and news seemed as remote as another planet. We were spending nearly 24 hours a day at his crib, getting by with brief naps in our hospital room.

Between constant interruptions for meds and monitor readings, our nurses coached Paulina on breast-feeding and taught us diapering and sponge-bathing. We learned to cuddle Andy around his intravenous tubes and monitor wires; we kissed him and sang to him.

Paulina mourned, "This is all wrong. We should be at home." But despite the unnatural setting she seemed like a natural mother. Her arms curved as if Andy had always rested there; his downy head fitted precisely into her cupped palms. Her voice softened and became more rhythmic when she talked to him, describing his room in our new apartment, with the blue sailboat border on the walls and shelves stacked with toys and tiny t-shirts. She recited the names of his grandparents, great-grandparents, aunts, uncles and cousins waiting to welcome him. *La familia*—it will be an expansive, resilient net, like a trampoline to catch and support him when he falls, or help him soar when he wants fly. Andy's dark gaze seemed to take in every word.

Bad blood

On day seven, the blood test results came back from the lab. Andy had a bacterial infection called *Listeria monocytogenes*. I was stunned. A blood infection? Wasn't the fever just a stress reaction?

"*Listeria's* not common and we're very lucky we found it," Dr. Maulen told us. "The antibiotic he's on will take care of it." But she couldn't tell us how Andy got the infection, and she briskly moved on to her other patients.

I wondered out loud if the blood test was accurate. "What if Dr. Maulen's making this up to save face—to justify this week in the hospital?"

"That's ridiculous, Andrés, you're overreacting. It's just an infection, and the medication is curing it, so everything will be fine." Paulina bent over Andy, sleeping in her arms. "Just fine."

"OK, we're totally new to this parenting business, what do we know about anything? Maybe it's not so unusual." The hospital didn't have Internet access, but I opened my laptop and plugged in a reference source I'd recently bought on a CD-ROM—*Scientific American Medicine*. I read that *Listeria* infection is very rare, but its infant mortality rate is greater than 80%. I decided not to share this with my wife.

Dr. Maulen wanted Andy to stay in the hospital for the remaining three days of the antibiotic. "But he looks fine—he hasn't had a fever since the first day," I protested.

Reluctantly, she agreed to let Andy finish the drugs orally at home, and she removed the IV from his hand. We dressed him in a pale blue outfit and nestled him in his portable Graco car seat. It would have been unthinkable to leave without saying a quick prayer of thanks in the hospital chapel. Prayer accompanies every event, large or small, in Mexican life, and we prayed as naturally as breathing.

Then we headed for home. We couldn't wait to put the last 10 days behind us.

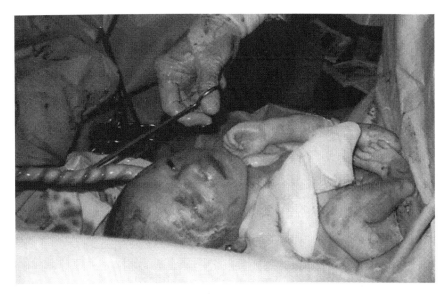

Andy's birth, May 15, 1999, Hospital Angeles, Mexico City.

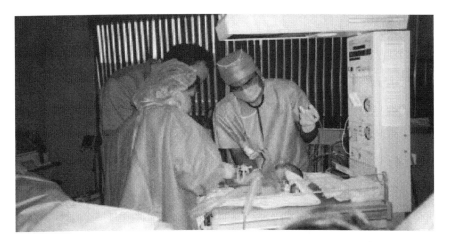

Andrés cutting the umbilical cord with Dr. Maulen.

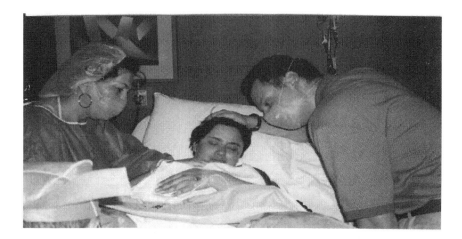

Dr. Maulen, Paulina, Andy and Andrés in the delivery room.

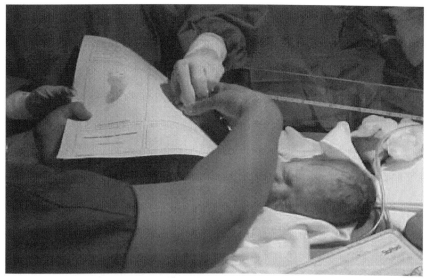

Andy fingerprints his birth certificate.

Constancia de Nacimiento

Nací en el Hospital Angeles de las Lomas

el 15 de Mayo de 1999

soy hij o de [illegible]

y de: [illegible]

[illegible]
Jefe del Cunero

Hospital Angeles de las Lomas

México, D.F. 24 de Mayo de 1999 Depto. de Cuna

Birth certificate – Hospital Angeles

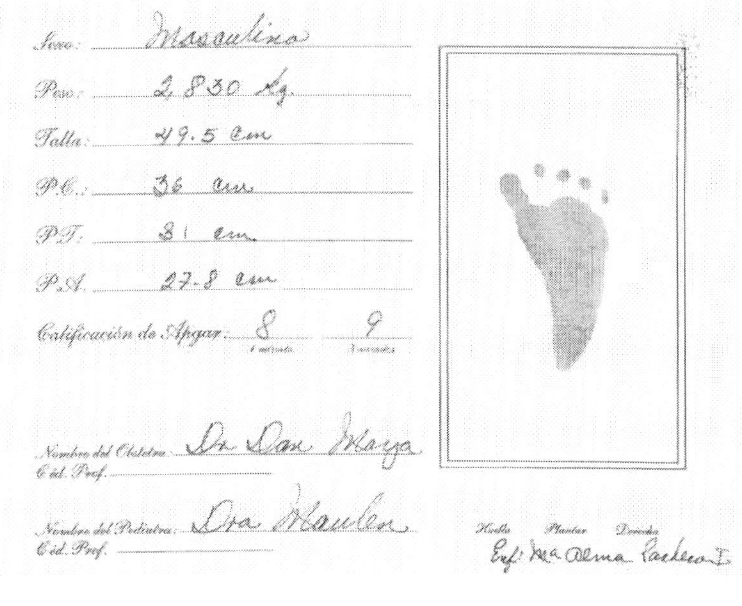

Sexo: Masculino

Peso: 2,830 Kg.

Talla: 49.5 cm

P.C.: 36 cm

P.T.: 31 cm

P.A. 27.8 cm

Calificación de Apgar: 8 (1 minuto) 9 (5 minutos)

Nombre del Obstetra: [illegible]
Céd. Prof.

Nombre del Pediatra: [illegible]
Céd. Prof.

Huella Plantar Derecha
Enf. [illegible]

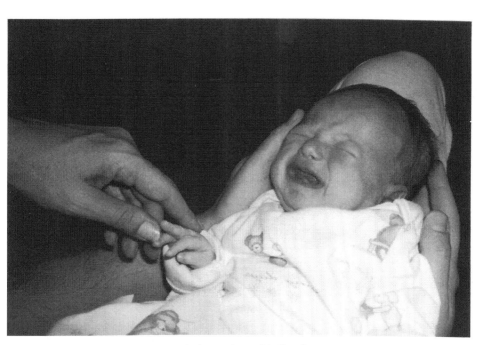

Andy reacting to his first fever.

Chapter Two
Home

When we walked in the door our place still smelled faintly of fresh paint. We'd been living with my parents for months while our new condo was renovated, and we'd finally moved in just two weeks before Andy was born. We hadn't gotten around to buying rugs or pictures or pots of hibiscus for the balcony. Only Andy's room was completely furnished, though we kept his bassinet in our room at night and jumped up every time he squeaked.

After a few days we began to relax. Like most middle-class Mexicans, we had a young woman to cook and clean, so Paulina was free to devote herself to Andy. I returned to work, sharing my introduction to fatherhood—I called it "extreme parenthood"—with my office colleagues. Then I stopped talking about it. I just wanted to get used to "normal parenthood."

Paulina's body recovered quickly from the birth and she looked more beautiful than ever, her small frame full and blooming. When she nursed Andy, she reminded me of the earthly Velásquez madonnas in the Mexico City art museum. Holding her close in bed, I recaptured the feeling I'd had since first falling in love with her. My unbelievable good fortune.

How we met

I'd first seen Paulina two-and-a-half years earlier, in December 1996, when I took charge of setting up a temporary branch office for Ekofon, my family's Mexico City telecommunications company. I'd been a company salesman for several years after graduate school. Now I was spending a year in Monterrey, developing a new territory in the northern provinces for our specialized business email services through a partnership with AT&T.

I knew the university nearby, Tec de Monterrey, would be a great source for the staff I needed. Browsing résumés in the Tec placement office, I found one that caught my attention: Ana Paulina d'Argence Zardain, 23, from Tuxtla Gutierrez, Chiapas. Her photo showed a pretty face with high cheekbones and lively, tilted eyes like Audrey Hepburn's. She was about to graduate with excellent grades and a business administration degree. I sneaked all 10 copies of her résumé out of her file folder so no one else could call her.

When she showed up for her interview she was even prettier than her photograph, wearing a tailored turquoise suit and pumps that showed off her legs. She was so petite her head barely reached the middle of my chest, but she shook hands firmly and proceeded to direct the interview with confidence. There was nothing I could do but offer her the office manager job on the spot.

Paulina and I organized the office quickly that winter, and our new customers kept us busy. I wanted to know her better, but she treated me with formality, and I heard her mention a boyfriend. Then I invited her on a one-day equipment-buying trip to Laredo, Texas. At the border, Paulina glanced over at my passport and exclaimed, "Andrés, you're only 25! Only two years older than I am!" And she stopped being so polite.

On the drive back from Laredo, we talked about our families. She'd grown up on a cattle ranch, a tomboy surrounded by cousins and horses and a vast, outdoor playground. *That explains her confidence*, I thought. Then we discovered our great-grandparents were from the same region of Spain—Asturias—and we each had a grandfather who was a coffee grower. As soon as I got home I called my *Abuelo* Mario, my mother's father. He remembered the Zardain name well. Paulina's grandfather had been a witness at my grandparents' wedding soon after both families had emigrated from Spain on the same boat in 1906. I couldn't wait to share the coincidence with Paulina. But she still kept her distance.

In late April, she mentioned she was visiting her parents' ranch down south in Chiapas for their big annual cattle show. It was on the same weekend I was flying south to Mexico City for my mother's¬—and my—birthday. (Mama always told me I was her most original birthday present ever.) That Friday, I gave Paulina a ride to the airport. On Sunday evening, waiting in the Mexico City airport for my return flight to Monterrey, I couldn't help checking to see how close her connection from Chiapas was. I quickly switched to the same 9 p.m. flight, and waited until the last minute to board the plane. No Paulina. I took one of the last two seats, my favorite spot right behind the cockpit where there's a little more room for legs like mine, but it didn't compensate for my disappointment. Just as the flight attendant was closing the door, Paulina, holding a wrapped parcel, raced down the jet way. Her eyes widened when she saw me. "What are you doing here? I thought your flight was hours ago!"

She took the seat next to mine and handed me the parcel, grinning. "Happy birthday, Andrés," she said. I laughed. She'd brought me the souvenirs her father gave to his cattle show customers¬—a box of Chiapas handicrafts and a big homemade cheese.

The flight passed in a dream. It was a clear night, with a full moon pouring silver over the *Cerro de la Silla*, Saddleback Mountain, below. We switched off the lights, and leaned back against the headrests with our faces turned toward each other. The moonlight deepened her eyes and polished her cheekbones. When our elbows brushed I felt a little electric thrill. We talked about our weekends and the work week ahead, but I kept thinking how beautiful she was, how much I liked her. Did she guess? Should I tell her?

I did tell her, 10 days later when I convinced her to let me take her out to dinner for her 24th birthday. The following week she returned the engagement ring her boyfriend had just given her. I already knew she was the one I wanted to spend my life with, and within a few months I proposed. Six months after that, on May 2, 1998, we danced at our wedding. Paulina looked like an angel in her strapless white gown and long veil. Peeping out beneath her skirt were custom-made platform shoes, giving her just enough height for dancing with me. We couldn't have been better matched.

We left the Monterrey office in charge of an associate, and we spent a few months working in a temporary San Francisco office, acquiring technical expertise for Mexico's impending voice-over-the-Internet services. Soon Paulina was pregnant. We moved back to Mexico City, and Andy arrived just 13 days after our first wedding anniversary.

Baptism

Now it was time for another celebration. A week after we came home from the hospital, I was wheeling a shopping cart through the cavernous Mexico City Costco with my father-in-law, *Don* Alfredo. He's been very successful in the cattle business and his fashionable wife shops at Neiman Marcus—but Alfredo loves a bargain and Costco is his kind of place.

"One case of Champagne will be enough," he suggested, examining a discounted box of Cuban cigars. I shook my head and hefted a second case of Moët & Chandon into the cart. Andy's baptism party, for about 40 family members, would be modest enough without stinting on the Champagne.

Church law requires a full baptismal mass. But until Andy grew stronger we were cautious about exposing him to many people, and after what we'd just been through, we didn't want to wait any longer to baptize him. So my grandfather Mario contacted a family friend, Father Salvador, the priest who had prepared me for my first communion. *Padre* "Chava" was a world traveler from Spanish Basque country, with a karate black belt and a smoker's gravelly voice, perfect for telling jokes. He agreed to perform the ceremony at our home, assuring us, "God will understand."

Under other circumstances, Andy's baptism would have been like the ones my older sister, Veronica, held for her kids. Each time, 200 guests gathered at my parents' weekend house in Cuernavaca. Every family member would attend, dressed in his or her best, filling the town cathedral. The godparents—*el Padrino y la Madrina*—stood at the font. (I got to be *el Padrino* for Veronica's first-born, Isabel). Next to them would be Vero and her husband, Juan, holding a solemn 6-month-old in a long, white embroidered dress, receiving the sacrament binding this child to our religion, our culture, and our family.

But that would be the only serious part. No people party like a big Mexican family and their friends, and baptisms offer the best excuse. Breakfast on my parents' terraced patio followed, a meal their *cocinera, Doña Leo*, would spend days preparing. Long linen-covered tables held trays of *enchiladas, huevos rancheros, frijoles refritos*, and my favorite, *chiles rellenos*—batter-fried poblano peppers stuffed with meat and cheese. Coffee from Casa Blanca, *Abuelo* Mario's plantation, filled steaming urns. My mother would show off her grandchild, now dressed in a second outfit and smiling for photographs. Women in fluttering silk dresses and high-heeled sandals would be sipping mimosas and rehashing family gossip under the bougainvillea. I'd join my dad, my older brother, also named Victor, and a cluster of men smoking celebratory cigars and drinking tequila shots. Teenagers waited on their grandmothers and aunts; younger kids ran underfoot, took a turn at the *piñata* or lined up at the dessert table for a slice of *pastel tres leches*. Then *Tío* Ricardo would bring out his guitar for everyone to sing pop tunes and folk songs long into the afternoon.

In contrast, Andy's baptism was a very scaled-down affair, held in our nearly empty dining room.   Paulina and I aren't especially religious, and we don't always agree with the Church.   But baptism is a life milestone as important as a wedding or funeral, and we both felt the solemnity of the event. Paulina was luminous in a silvery-gray silk shift and pearls—with her short-cropped hair and serious eyes she looked like a young novitiate. At 17 days old, Andy was so small the only family christening robe that fit was his great-grandmother's, from a time when newborns were baptized within days because they so often died within weeks. *Padre* Chava used a large crystal salad bowl as a baptismal font. "May his difficult beginning be a blessing in disguise to help strengthen him for life." My son slept through the blessing and the trickle of holy water on his head. I drank three glasses of Moët, but couldn't quite summon that festive feeling.

* * *

We didn't know what a tortuous road stretched ahead—how our baby would suffer and how we'd suffer with him. We didn't know he'd spend nearly 1,000 days in seven different hospitals, see more than 300 doctors and swerve close to death many times. We didn't know how our faith in God, medicine and ourselves would be tested, and how we'd have to take matters into our own hands to find the medical miracle that would save him.

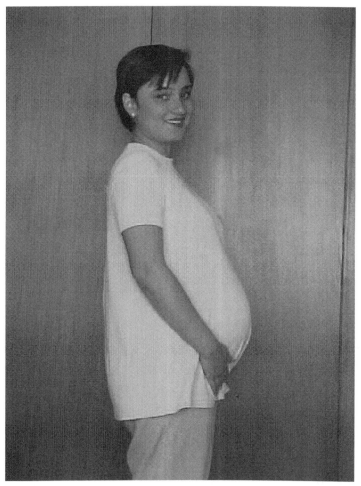

Paulina's pregnancy profile.

Baptism at home: Padre Salvador, Andy, Paulina, Andrés and Marilu.

Andrés, Andy and Paulina visiting Cuernavaca.

Chapter Three
Setbacks

At four weeks, Andy was sleeping well, breastfeeding eagerly and entertaining a steady stream of visitors. His diminutive perfection continued to amaze me. I loved to cradle him along my forearm, his heels tucked in the crook of my elbow and his head in my hand as he stared at my face. At his one-month check-up, Dr. Maulen said he was developmentally right on target.

But one night soon after, Andy woke with diarrhea and a temperature and wouldn't stop crying. At dawn we called Dr. Maulen, who told us to come straight to the hospital. I fought a sinking feeling.

In the lab for a blood draw and stool sample, Paulina held Andy tight as he screamed at the needle prick. Within hours we learned he had "occult" blood in his diaper, which we couldn't detect but the lab tests could. His white blood cell count was elevated—a sign of infection, Dr. Maulen explained, probably gastro-intestinal given the blood in his stool. He'd have to be re-admitted to the hospital for further tests and at least a week of intravenous antibiotics. My sinking feeling grew to Titanic proportions—how could this be happening again?

As Paulina struggled to absorb this news and soothe Andy, I turned to my laptop to read about white blood cells. In the army of components making up the human immune system, they're part of the advance guard, cruising through the blood stream on alert. They respond to signals that an invading organism is present by rushing to an infection site. They can leave the bloodstream and migrate into the tissues, where they multiply quickly. Like morphing Terminators, they surround, ingest and kill alien bacteria or viruses, often dying themselves in the process. These cells are also called leukocytes, and when their numbers increase in the blood, "an elevated leukocyte count," it indicates infection.

By evening, Andy had a new tube in his arm and, exhausted from screaming, fell asleep in his hospital crib. I had an inflatable mattress next to him, but for a while Paulina and I both squeezed onto the sofa where she would sleep.

We held each other and asked, what had we done wrong? Weren't we clean enough? Had we exposed him to too many visitors?

A new bug

We re-entered hospital life like a bad dream. With his infection, Andy couldn't be around other babies on the pediatric floor, but the nurses on this floor didn't have any experience with infants. At each daily blood draw, Paulina held a shrieking Andy as a grim-faced nurse poked and pricked, trying to find a thread-like vein.

On the fourth day Dr. Maulen appeared with the results from the lab: Andy's intestinal infection was caused by an organism called *Escherichia coli*. "The antibiotic he's on will take care of it by the end of the week," she said. "*E. coli* bacteria are everywhere, it's a normal part of your intestinal flora, but some strains create a dangerous toxin. That seems to be what he's picked up."

"But *how*?" I asked.

She seemed unwilling to admit she didn't know. "It could be from any number of sources..."

The unanswered question rattled in the back of my mind as the week dragged on, and my *Scientific American Medicine* files on *E. coli* didn't enlighten me much. Paulina didn't want to speculate with me. She was intent on watching the antibiotic take effect, and on distracting Andy from nurses with needles.

He lay in the hospital crib, taking up only a fraction of its real estate. We hung his favorite toy on the rail—a Fisher Price wind-up full of cascading plastic beads. It sounded like a waterfall and lasted exactly 13 minutes. He'd cry when it stopped, so we must have cranked that thing a hundred times a day. By the fifth day Andy rewarded us—his very first smile.

For a while, nothing else mattered. We discovered our capacity for goofiness—we made faces and talked in funny voices and played music—anything to see that sweet, open-mouthed reply. I watched Paulina light up whenever he cooed back at us and I wondered how babies do it. How can a nine-pound 6-week-old evoke such huge feelings? Surely we were capable of protecting this small person, this joy, forever.

When the week was up, we consented to one last blood test to assure Dr. Maulen that his infection-fighting army had done its job and was "standing down." Then we escaped.

We returned to our welcoming apartment, walking from room to room, lifting shades and opening balcony doors to the languid late-June air. Our *cocinera* prepared a wonderful meal—chicken *flautas* with *guacamole* and sour cream. Paulina fed Andy, seated in the rocking chair in his bedroom. Then he fell asleep in his own canopied crib like a little prince, splayed on his back, arms open as though expecting a gift. In the privacy of our own bed, we embraced with fierce hunger, releasing the tightly wound spring of the last seven days.

More bad news

The next morning, Dr. Maulen called—the blood test showed Andy's leukocytes were still elevated and she wanted us to meet her at the hospital for a consultation. I nearly threw the phone down. "She's crazy! No way am I letting those nurses near him again!"

"Please, calm down!" begged Paulina. "If he's still infected, we're lucky she found it." She took my arm. "Andrés, this is scaring me. We need to trust the doctor."

I was scared, too. Also angry and frustrated. For Paulina's sake, I tried to control myself.

My parents accompanied us back to the hospital while Paulina's mother, Lupita, who'd just arrived to visit us, stayed behind with Andy.

Dr. Maulen's expression was pinched, like the night after Andy's birth. Frowning, she said, "It's just not normal for a baby to have a blood infection and then a gastrointestinal tract infection in his first weeks of life. A normal leukocyte count is 10,000 to 15,000; your son's measures 30,000. I'm afraid the high count means his white blood cells still aren't working properly, but I can't say how."

I suddenly felt nauseated. I envisioned Andy's blood cells marching to battle with faulty weapons, calling for reinforcements who had no weapons at all, and everyone falling against bigger guns. How could this essential function not work?

Then Dr. Maulen described a disease she'd read about recently, in children who had elevated leukocytes and chronic infections. Some kind of immune deficiency.

"And do you think Andy has this? How is it treated?" I demanded.

She took a deep breath, tossed back her shoulder-length hair. "There's no known treatment."

I felt rising fear. Here was the chief of the pediatric ICU, telling us our son could have a very rare disease with no cure.

"Could this be a reaction to all the infections he's had? The huge amounts of antibiotics?" I asked her. My heart was thudding so hard it made my voice unsteady.

Dr. Maulen paused, then said, "I don't know." I could see how much she hated those words.

Paulina said, "But he's looking so well right now, he was laughing with my mom when we left the apartment..." She was on the verge of tears and I put my arm around her.

"Well, what are our options, what do you recommend?" I asked.

"I have two options for you," she answered. "You can go to the United States to look for a specific diagnosis and treatment. I could go with you, if you want. Or you can stay here and I can call in local specialists to see your son."

"Do you know someone in the US who could help us?" I asked. She didn't, just recommended Houston as the nearest US pediatric hospital. I went out into the hallway with Paulina and my parents.

My mother, the positive, upbeat authoritative matriarch of our family, looked deeply distressed. "I'm not sure this doctor knows what she's doing," she said. "Why can't she find what's wrong?"

"Andrés, take both options," my father said calmly. "Once we consult with doctors here, we could contact US specialists by email or even do a video conference. There's no sense in going to Houston if we don't know any doctors there." He didn't need to mention the other big factor: Our insurance covered only Mexican healthcare.

We returned to Dr. Maulen's office and told her we wanted to see the best specialists in Mexico and get advice from best specialists in the United States.

We brought Andy back to the hospital on Monday morning. "No more needles, no poking!" I told the nurses. "He's here just to see a few doctors."

Dr. Maulen first phoned Texas Children's Hospital in Houston, where the consulting doctor said the high leukocytes could be a holdover from all the past infections and could stabilize with time. He didn't think it was necessary to bring the patient to Houston, just continue the antibiotics. Oh, and had we considered a lumbar puncture?

"That's a spinal tap, where we use a needle to extract and examine spinal fluid," explained Dr. Maulen. "It's a test for meningitis, a brain and nervous system infection, but your son doesn't have any meningitis symptoms. His fontanelle—the soft spot in his skull—would be hard and bulging in that case."

Then she called in several Mexican immunologists, who examined Andy one by one while he gurgled and smiled at all the attention. They all said the same thing: his white blood cells were probably still showing a reaction to recent infection. We wanted nothing more than to believe them, so we went home.

But it took only a week for Andy to develop a third fever.

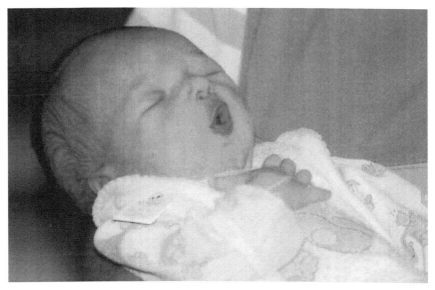

Andy with Paulina at home.

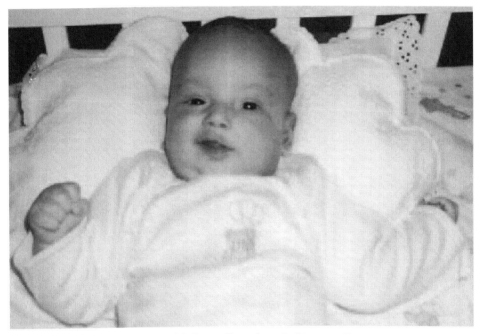

Andy's first smile, at home in his own crib.

Chapter Four
Kretschmer

"You can use either me or your other pediatrician, but not both. If I take your case, I have my own team." We were sitting in the office of Dr. Roberto Kretschmer, a pediatric immunologist recommended by Dr. Maulen as simply "the best."

Dr. Kretschmer was a tall man in his 60s with a big paunch and gruff manners, though his huge glasses gave his face a benign look. He was apparently accustomed to giving orders, and during our interview he kept pressing the button on his intercom and bawling instructions to his assistant. It was our second visit in as many days, and already I liked his tart observations and sense of command.

Yesterday, he'd ordered more blood tests from his own on-site laboratory while we related Andy's history. Dr. Kretschmer didn't believe the *Listeria* diagnosis.

"The Hospital Angeles lab is not equipped to find this type of bacteria. And I'm not talking about their fancy equipment; I'm talking about the staff. That hospital is full of doctors who are more concerned about wearing Hermès ties than taking care of patients. And they don't do research there—without research you can't give the best clinical care."

"Dr. Kretschmer's kind of a bully," Paulina had said to me last night. But today she was distracted, sitting in a corner, trying to comfort our crying baby.

I glanced at the framed diplomas on his office wall:

UNIVERSIDAD NACIONAL AUTONOMA DE MEXICO

UNIVERSITY OF CHICAGO

HARVARD MEDICAL SCHOOL:

CHILDREN'S HOSPITAL BOSTON

I had no qualms about giving up Dr. Maulen.

"Dr. Maulen told us we need a leukocyte function test. You're our last resort," I answered. "You're Andy's pediatrician from now on."

He shook my hand. "Good. I'm sending you to a different hospital, the Centro Médico ABC, for the leukocyte test," he said. "Dr. Claudia Vazquez is head of the pediatric unit there—she'll take care of you."

Then he called Dr. Vazquez, leaning back in his chair and rubbing his forehead as he told her, from memory, every detail of Andy's story. I heard him order a spinal tap to rule out meningitis, and I didn't question it—I don't know why, but I trusted this guy. Kretschmer sent us home with his own private phone number. "Hope for the best and act for the worst," he said, shaking hands again.

We arrived at Centro Médico ABC early the next morning. Despite its excellent reputation, the hospital's located in Observatorio, one of Mexico City's most crime-ridden districts. It only increased our sense of dread to see the abandoned streets, the police patrolling the parking lot, the guards at the entrance.

It had been a bad night; Andy cried himself to exhaustion and kept closing his eyes and turning away from light as though it pained him. Paulina and I were bleary-eyed ourselves. While Dr. Vazquez examined Andy she made a few pointed comments to let us know her hospital was better than Hospital Angeles, with a more professional lab and more experienced nurses who wore "real uniforms." Then she admitted us to the pediatric floor—about eight rooms and a bone marrow transplant unit for cancer patients. We waited in a darkened room for the neonatologist, a military doctor named Dr. Martínez-Natera.

He knocked once and turned on the light. Andy winced and squeezed his eyes shut. "I'm here to do the lumbar puncture. Pleasure to meet you." Dr. Martínez-Natera wore spit-shined shoes and spoke in staccato; the nurses jumped at his every word.

"We're going to take him to the treatment room, he'll be back in 45 minutes. I'll insert a needle in his spine to extract some fluid —if it's cloudy it means there's a brain infection. Give him a kiss if you like."

Brain infection?? Wait! I wanted to slow him down.

"Where is that treatment room? How big is the needle?"

"It's two doors away and don't worry about the size of the needle. Give him a kiss, he'll do fine."

One of the nurses took Andy from Paulina's arms—her hands dropped to her sides and she sagged a little. "Can't I go with him?"

"Are we allowed in there?" I asked.

"Oh no!" the nurse told me. "We'll let you know when we're finished."

But I followed her anyway, to a small room next to the nurses' station, where the doctor was waiting in a mask and gloves. I glimpsed the straps and netting that would hold Andy down on the table—there was no general anesthesia. Andy was already crying as the door closed on me, and his screams grew louder. I knew Paulina was sobbing back in our room. I wanted to be the one getting the needle, but all I could do was lean against the wall and pray. Another father walked by in the hallway and nodded at me. "The torture room…" he said. I learned that in 50 minutes you can say 1,437 Hail Marys.

Andy came out with a new tube in his arm, tears still on his cheeks.

"Your son has meningitis. He needs a 21-day antibiotic treatment," said Dr. Martínez-Natera in his rapid-fire way. "I recommend a catheter and central line to administer the medication intravenously." He explained it was the best way to deliver the antibiotics, through a thin tube inserted through Andy's tiny vein to his heart. He'd do the procedure himself the next day.

Paulina's face fell, but I felt a shadow of relief I couldn't explain. Maybe there was a chance it had been meningitis all along, and we'd finally know why Andy was so sick.

After Dr. Martínez-Natera left, Paulina and I sat in Andy's room as he slept, and tried to repeat the doctor's exact words to make sure we both understood. "He said the fluid was cloudy, right? He said something about a tube that gets placed directly in his heart?" We clutched each other, terrified.

"We have to tell our parents," Paulina groaned.

It took extra effort to keep updating friends and family, to respond to everyone's opinions and advice, their prayers, their weeping. These hospitalizations were anguishing for our parents, but things were moving so fast it was hard to share the latest development before we had to decipher and explain another medical concept. We needed more than sympathy and support. We needed answers.

At 2:00 a.m., Dr. Kretschmer knocked on the door, turned on the lights and announced, "I always visit at this hour. It's when my patients feel most alone."

Only if they're awake, I thought, as we struggled out of deep sleep. Still, I was glad to see him.

"The plan right now is to start the antibiotics while we wait for the meningitis cultures from the lab. Your baby needs to be in the hospital for a minimum of three weeks to clear the infection from his central nervous system, and he'll be getting a catheter for these medications. We'll have time later to do the leukocyte test, but not until we stabilize him. First things first."

"The catheter sounds so drastic. Can't he take the antibiotics orally?"

"The dose he needs would damage his digestive system."

He approached the sleeping baby and with big, gentle hands measured Andy's head with a yellow measuring tape, showing us the unmistakably bulging fontanelle—a meningitis hallmark. Not that we needed more evidence.

At 5:00 a.m. there were more opening doors and clicking lights. "Good morning, I'm ready to put his catheter in," Dr. Martínez-Natera said briskly. Paulina wept again as Andy was taken from her arms and carried off to the torture room.

I paced the hallway for an hour as nurses passed in their starched uniforms, looking like something out of a 1960s TV medical drama. When Andy returned, limp from screaming, a tiny cylinder protruded from his arm, surrounded by stitches and transparent tape.

"We just need to take an x-ray to check that the catheter tip is hanging correctly inside his heart," said Dr. Martínez-Natera. "Don't let any of these nurses touch this. I'll personally take care of it."

I looked at the device in Andy's arm, visualizing the hair-thin, hollow wire snaking through a vein smaller than a spaghetti strand all the way into his heart. *Oh my God. What if it rips, what if it damages his heart?* I forced myself to breathe, to remain calm, afraid my face betrayed me.

"Can I pick him up, Doctor? Is it OK if we hold him?" Paulina asked with effort. She met my eyes, then looked away. I understood. Focusing on Andy, not our own fear, was the only way we could handle this.

Hard lessons

Meningitis takes three weeks to treat: 21 days; 504 hours; 30,240 minutes. Our hospital room was white and featureless, and the only visual relief was the window. It overlooked a warehouse, and I had a clear view of its low-rent security system. A wooden mannequin holding a fake rifle glided slowly from window to window on a mechanized track, completing a circuit about every half hour. He and I had something in common—we were both going nowhere.

Andy was hooked up to a complex plumbing system—electric pumps and tubes infusing fluids and medication into his little body. The pumps beeped every time the fluid sank to a certain level, forcing us to call in a nurse to fiddle with knobs and adjust the flow. Every 40 minutes, the same routine. We'd push the call button and get the nurses' station:

"What do you need?"

"The pump is beeping again."

"I'll send your nurse in."

Then the loudspeaker, "Lucy, room 429, Lucy..." throughout the floor. In would come Lucy to fix the pump.

It was the same procedure for a diaper change.

"What do you need?"

"Diapers, please."

"Lucy..." bleated the PA system.

In she'd come with a single diaper, to be recorded individually on our account. The routines were so disruptive Paulina had to abandon breastfeeding and pumping milk, and Andy was switched to Enfamil formula.

He began to improve after a few days on the meds, and we tried to keep him amused. At home he'd begun to reach for toys, but now he was tethered by so many tubes he couldn't move freely. He lay on his back in his crib, gravely studying his Fisher-Price wind-up toy for hours.

Paulina and I divided up our time so one of us would always be with him. She spent 12-hour days and I took the night shift after work and a brief nap. Paulina would get tearful at the evening changing of the guard. It was a 45-minute trip home, and I hated having her drive through Observatorio alone. "When will we ever have time together, to ourselves?" she mumbled into my chest as I held her tight. "A nice dinner, a movie, a date? The last time we danced was at our wedding." Fifteen months ago—it seemed like decades.

"Soon. Soon we'll all be home. Now go home and get some sleep."

For me, an overnight in the hospital meant very little rest, even if Andy slept. One night as I was lying on the sofa in the dark, a nurse entered to set up the antibiotic pump. Andy was finally out cold, and I prayed she wouldn't wake him as she adjusted the pump and left. I don't know how long I dozed, lulled by the pump's rhythmic *whoosh-click-click*. Suddenly I jerked awake. The room was black except for the pump's tiny green and red blinking lights. I heard Andy breathing as I felt my way to his crib to check that his IV tubes weren't twisted. I touched the mattress—it was soaked. Was his diaper leaking? I switched on the lamp next to the bed and my heart jumped.

What the hell?!

Andy lay in a puddle of blood, lurid against the white sheets.

I frantically punched the call button, trying not to raise my voice. *"¡Emergencia! ¡Necesito una enfermera aquí ahorita!* Emergency! I need a nurse in here *now!"* Then I saw it—the knob on one of his infusion tubes was open, allowing blood to flow *out* of his body, where it dripped from his catheter all over the crib. I twisted the knob once and the flow stopped, just as the nurse who'd last fixed the pump entered the room. "That valve was left open!" I hissed. "He's bleeding—call the doctor!"

"¡Dios!" The nurse scurried for help as Andy woke and started to cry. I lifted him with shaking hands, his tubes trailing, a line of blood drops spattering the floor. I held him against my chest and rocked him while my heart hammered.

The doctor strode in, a young resident I'd seen on the floor a few times. "We'll need a blood draw to check his levels," he said.

"What?! You want to take *more* blood?" I was incredulous. And furious.

"Well, umm…" He pinched Andy's fingers and feet and checked his color. "He looks OK," he said. "I don't think he lost too much blood—it just looks like more than it is. He doesn't need a transfusion¬, he'll be fine." He stifled a yawn, avoided meeting my eyes, and left the room.

It was all I could do not to follow and strangle him, and the guilty nurse as well when she came back with clean sheets. I turned away with Andy in my arms when she reached for him—I didn't want her near him. Tight-mouthed, she left the room.

I sponged Andy until the water in the basin was deep pink; I put him in a fresh diaper and t-shirt without disturbing his tubes. He was sleepy and compliant. Then I changed my own stained shirt and sat next to the crib. I tried to clear my mind, but over and over I saw the room spring from darkness into light, revealing my son in a bloody pool.

When Paulina arrived in the morning, I waited until she settled in to give Andy his bottle. Then I told her what had happened, my chest tightening all over again. Her eyes widened and she clutched Andy so close he let out a little cry and let go of the nipple. "He could have bled to death!"

"I don't know why I woke up when I did," I said. "Maybe I smelled the blood?" Suddenly, I was so tired I could have dropped to the floor. She glanced at the baby as he resumed his bottle with little humming sounds, his eyes on her face.

"It must have been a guardian angel." She looked up at me and her expression grew fierce. "We can never leave him alone even for a minute. Never."

I exhaled. "Never."

Our belief in medicine—and practitioners—was about to be shaken further. The first spinal tap identified *Streptococcus bovis* bacteria, which *Scientific American Medicine* considered an extremely rare cause for meningitis. I was suspicious. At the next weekly lumbar puncture the test came back showing a new bug, *Staphylococcus warnieri*. Dr. Martínez-Natera declared it must have been a contaminated sample.

"How do we know the first one wasn't contaminated too?" I asked. "What if the third one shows something entirely different?" No reply.

The more I looked, the more inconsistencies and incompetence I found. I knew Paulina wanted to believe in our doctors, but I discovered most of them would rather keep you in the dark than say, "I don't know." When Andy woke one morning with a yellow discharge gluing his eyes shut, the arrogant young resident had to consult three other doctors to diagnose a staph infection. "Probably from the air conditioning," he said, but I knew he didn't have a clue.

I became every doctor's nightmare, the parent who reads everything he can find about each test or treatment and who questions every procedure. The more bumbling the medical profession seemed, the easier it was to blame them for everything happening to my son. But I was desperate for someone to trust. That someone turned out to be Roberto Kretschmer.

Teamwork

Kretschmer was the man with the plan, and the only one who shared his thoughts with me and answered my endless questions. He continued his

2 a.m. visits, his belly preceding him through the door, his booming voice waking us all. Paulina warmed to him, especially when he handled Andy. He'd take off his glasses, pick the baby up tenderly to say hello, holding Andy against his huge face. "*¿Cómo está mi amigo?* And how's my little friend?"

Then he'd draw me diagrams to explain the next test. "Look, here's how antibodies work," he'd say. "Remember the white blood cells, the leukocytes? There are other types of cells in the immune system, like B-lymphocytes. As soon as these B-cells detect an antigen—meaning something foreign like a bacteria or virus—they mature into plasma cells, and produce protein molecules called antibodies. The B-lymphocytes know how to make antibodies to virtually any foreign micro-organism in our environment, but only the appearance of an antigen prompts them to "grow up" and put that knowledge to work. Now, there are four different chemical antibody types, connected to specific areas and functions of the body, and the beauty of it is, each type can produce proteins that precisely fit an antigen like a key in a lock. The polio antibody fits the poliovirus; the diphtheria antibody fits the diphtheria bacterium, etc. As soon as the antibody clicks into the antigen, it secretes a substance that either inactivates the bacteria or virus, or coats it to enable leukocytes to gobble it up easily. But even more amazing, the long life and memory of B-lymphocytes enables us to retain immunity to viruses and bacteria that infected us many years ago. For example, once you've been infected with chicken pox, you're unlikely to catch it again. Your B-cells can remember. Elegant, no?"

Yes, I marveled.

Kretschmer went ahead with Andy's leukocyte function test, in which I served as a control patient. A technician scraped a spot on our right arms, and then tested the raw, oozing patches for white blood cells rushing to defend the wound site. My leukocytes showed up, Andy's did not.

"Absence of proof is not a proof of absence," said Dr. Kretschmer. And he was right; when the test was repeated, Andy's white blood cells responded. Kretschmer noted that Andy's eye infection also showed his leukocytes were slaying invaders—the yellowish discharge was the battle's cellular debris.

Other tests followed. We learned Andy had plenty of antibodies. His bone marrow was producing healthy amounts of blood cells. He tested negative for AIDS, herpes and Epstein-Barr viruses. His immune system *must* be working.

Before every procedure, Kretschmer told us, "Hope for the best and act for the worst." We were a team—his job was to find the diagnosis; to name the enemy. Our job was to keep urging the other doctors and nurses to give Andy their best care. And to watch their every move.

After three weeks the meningitis had cleared and Dr. Kretschmer couldn't think of any more tests. We reviewed all the results together; some were conclusive, others uncertain or contradictory, but it seemed that Andy's immune response functioned. All the infections? "Could be just spectacular bad luck," Kretschmer said, with a look I'd come to recognize. There were still questions in his mind. "We have a saying in medical school, 'If you hear hoofbeats, think horses, not zebras,'" he said. "The right answer is most often the obvious one. But in your son's case, Señor Treviño, I'm thinking giraffes." He asked us to show up in his clinic in five days to discuss the routine immunizations Andy should be starting soon.

I saluted the wooden guard in the warehouse across the street from the window in Andy's room. We donated some toys to the nurses' station for other patients, and once again we headed home. As I drove through the desolate streets of Observatorio, with Andy asleep in the car seat, Paulina said quietly, "Dr. Kretschmer doesn't really think it's just bad luck, does he." I couldn't respond. I was clinging to the test results because it's all we had. Because I wanted to be done with lingering doubt. Then Paulina added, her voice sober, "Well, I choose to believe the tests. I can't go forward otherwise."

I rested my hand on her knee. "Agreed."

More giraffes

It was late August and we'd missed summer's fiestas and parties; the weekends at my parents' villa in Cuernavaca; the beach vacations with relatives in Akumal. But Paulina and I were grateful just to be home reveling in the smallest domestic graces— a home-cooked meal, baby bath time, our own bed. With renewed energy, I returned to work, where I was designing the company website. Paulina was ready to enjoy some of the pleasures of motherhood.

To mark a new beginning, I took the last of my savings and with *Don* Alfredo's help, bought Paulina a car of her own. Her father had wanted to buy her a Dodge Neon, but I did some research and chose something different. It was a Mercedes Class A hatchback, a great little inexpensive car made in Brazil and sold only in Latin America. When I handed her the keys, the look on her face was worth every peso. Now she could take Andy to the park, to lunch with friends, to visit her aunt Ana José. And go to doctor's appointments.

In mid-September, Andy was 4 months old, rolling over, grabbing his toys and laughing at his own baby jokes. Dr. Kretschmer suggested we start vaccinations, though he still had enough doubts about Andy's leukocyte reaction to be wary of using the live oral polio virus that was standard in Mexico. "We need to get the de-activated Salk vaccine they use in the US." He handed me a prescription written in English on an old pad with a US address: 300 Longwood Avenue, Boston, Massachusetts.

My mother-in-law, Lupita, found us a contact, a pharmacist from Monterrey who made frequent trips back and forth across the border with his car trunk full of American medications. He Fed-Exed them around Mexico for a nice profit. We ordered the injectable Salk vaccine and waited for the smuggler's next trip.

Paulina phoned me at the office one afternoon a few days later, panic in her voice. "I've changed Andy's diaper 15 times today! I've called every mother I know for advice on diarrhea. Should I call Dr. Kretschmer? I'm sure he'll think I'm just another hysterical new mom, but it's getting worse and I'm scared."

Back to Kretschmer's clinic. The first set of lab tests were negative for intestinal infection, but Andy didn't improve, so in a couple of days Dr. Kretschmer sent us to another lab an hour across town to test for a more rare bacteria, *clostridium difficile*. While we waited for the results we spent a worried weekend trying to get Andy to eat or drink. By Monday morning, he was running a fever and crying without tears. When Kretschmer examined him, gently pinching a skin fold on Andy's little belly, he said, "Oh yes, he's dehydrated—see how his skin stays pinched? You're going back to Centro Médico ABC, little man."

Paulina and I could barely look at each other as the ground opened and swallowed the last few weeks' fragile contentment. I felt too numb to do anything but follow orders.

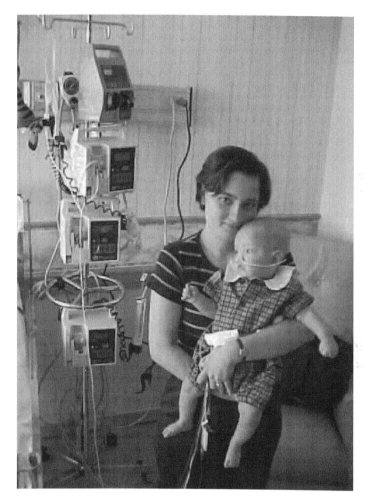

Andy and Paulina at Hospital ABC.

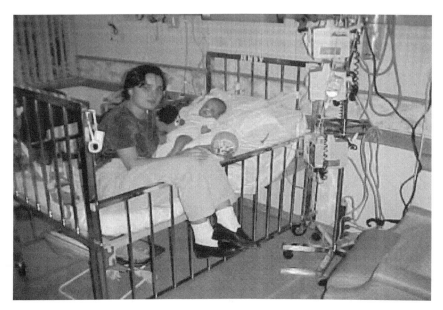

Andy and Paulina at Hospital ABC.

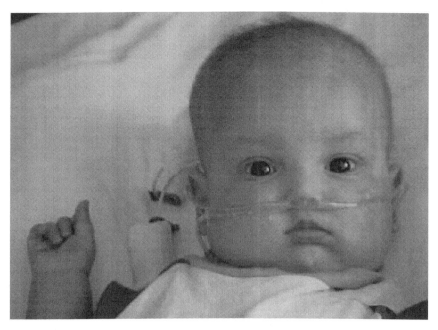

Andy with a central line and oxygen tube, Hospital ABC.

Andy and Dr. Kretschmer at Hospital ABC.

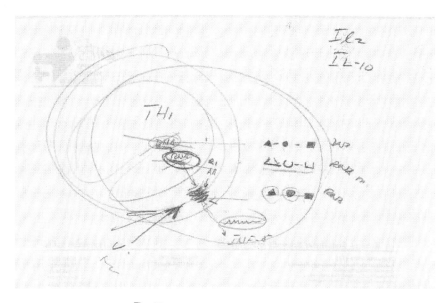

Dr. Kretschmer's notes and sketches.

Chapter Five
Hospital as Home

Our new room at ABC faced east, with a view across Mexico City's smog-layered expanse to the twin peaks on the horizon, *Popocatepetl* and *Iztaccíhuatl*. *Popocatepetl*, "smoking mountain," is an active volcano, regularly rumbling and raining ash. According to Aztec mythology, the warrior *Popoca* was in love with the beautiful *Iztaccíhuatl*. Her father, the emperor, sent *Popoca* to war, hoping to prevent their union, then falsely told *Izta* her lover had fallen in battle. She died of grief, and when *Popoca* returned, he lay by *Izta's* grave until he died, too. The pitying gods changed them into mountains. *Iztaccíhuatl* is known as *La Mujer Dormida*, "the sleeping woman," for her undulating curves. The gods gave *Popoca's* peak an inextinguishable torch with which to guard his beloved. As I gazed out at *Popocatepetl's* white plume, evidence of latent tantrums, I understood the rage that comes from being unable to protect those you love.

At 2 a.m., Dr. Kretschmer lumbered into our hospital room, saying, "Absence of proof is not a proof of absence—the test shows it's definitely *C. difficile*. It's a bacteria common in hospitals, often shows up in people who've been on antibiotics for an extended period. It was hiding from us all last week. How's my little friend?" Andy woke, whimpered, then stopped as Kretschmer lifted him in his big, capable hands.

Kretschmer had prescribed a drug called Flagyl, but the diarrhea was relentless and sometimes we found blood in Andy's diapers. I pictured the bacteria eating holes in my son's stomach. After 10 days of refusing to eat, Andy was pale and losing weight, subsisting on intravenous fluids. Kretschmer recommended a gastroenterologist, Dr. Madrazo, who might have a better idea of how to treat the diarrhea. But when we contacted him, Dr. Madrazo told us he was leaving for an Acapulco medical convention, and fobbed us off on an associate who seemed totally unconcerned that Andy hadn't improved.

Vancomycin express

Searching the web, I found the three treatment options for *C. difficile*, the most recommended being Vancomycin, an antibiotic that kills bacteria only in the intestine. When I pointed this out to the gastroenterology associate, he said, "Hmmm. Vancomycin might be a good option if Flagyl isn't working. But the intravenous form doesn't work with *C. difficile*, and there's no oral Vancomycin in Mexico. I'll see you on rounds tomorrow and we'll talk further."

I felt like grabbing and shaking him. If he knew Andy needed medication that wasn't available here, why not immediately start looking for it in the US? Seething, I left Paulina and Andy in the hospital room and drove to Kretschmer's office.

I sat with him alone for the first time, no baby crying in the background. He handed me a US prescription for the oral drug, written on the pad with the Boston address, and paid me his gruff equivalent of a compliment. "You seem to be a dad who knows his way around—I'm sure you'll find a way to get the Vancomycin from the States."

He rocked back in his swivel chair, hands folded on his stomach, and told me he was consulting a colleague in the Mexican national vaccine program about any possible connection between Andy's elevated leukocytes and the diarrhea. He was also considering giving Andy a shot of gamma globulin—a kind of antibody—because he'd read it might help this kind of intestinal flux. And when the *C. difficile* infection cleared we should consider going to one of his pediatric immunology colleagues in Denver or Chicago or Boston, where immune tests and gastroenterology treatments were more advanced. "Your son's condition is a mystery. But we'll get to the bottom of it."

I absorbed every word and felt a clenched place in my chest release. Years ago, I'd taken the SCUBA certification with Juan, who was to become my sister Veronica's husband. Juan and Vero used to take me along as the kid brother chaperone on weekend trips to a cousin's hotel at the beach in Akumal. I'm forever grateful to Juan for introducing me to diving, to a magical undersea world. And I'll never forget the day we were exploring a cave 80 feet down, when my oxygen tank ran dry. Before I could panic, Juan grabbed me and gave me the extra respirator hose hooked to his tank. He kept his eyes fixed on my face as we slowly rose to the surface.

Now I listened to Kretschmer's deep, authoritative voice and realized I'd been holding my breath for a long time.

Meanwhile, Andy still couldn't eat, he was feverish and vomiting bile. The blood in his diaper was worse. The nurses had no suggestions, just observed that Andy's belly was distended. Paulina was frantic, sponging him with cool towels, trying to get him to take a bottle, switching to soy formula. I made nipples out of sterile rubber gloves, even tried filling his pacifier with formula, but Andy seemed too weak to suck. When the gastroenterology associate came by, I cut off his pointless comments and said, "It's time to switch him to oral Vancomycin now. The Flagyl isn't working."

"Sounds like good idea, if you can find it," the associate said.

You're supposed to be the one with the ideas! I couldn't hide my disgust.

It was too late that Friday to order Vancomycin from the smuggler contact in Monterrey. I called my brother, Victor, who was living in Los Angeles at the time. If I faxed him the prescription from Kretschmer, he promised to find the Vancomycin and send it from Tijuana at the border.

The next afternoon, my brother walked into our hospital room, with a box in his hands and a smile on his face. "Did someone order oral Vancomycin?" He'd flown with the medicine all the way from L.A

Six years my senior, Victor's the kind of guy who wakes up smiling every day. He's also a natural entrepreneur. At 16, he started selling fresh fruit to my mother's friends in our Mexico City neighborhood, using the proceeds to buy his first car, a '62 Chevy. After college, he co-founded the family business with my dad. Victor's someone I've looked up to all my life, but I'd never been so glad to see him. Paulina jumped up and threw her arms around him. His smile faded when he looked at Andy.

I quickly translated the English instructions so the nurses could administer the medication orally with a dropper. We watched as Andy swallowed, praying it would work.

New Enemies

The weeks dragged on. Kretschmer ordered Andy switched to total parenteral nutrition, or TPN —an intravenous tube delivering nutrients directly into his blood stream. Our friend Dr. Martínez-Natera installed another catheter, in Andy's other arm. "Can't use the same vein twice," he explained. It was scary to think that veins were a nonrenewable resource. The plan was to supplement the intravenous nutrients with formula through a feeding tube in his nose that went to his stomach. The white plastic tubing was threaded into Andy's nose, down his throat to his stomach.

With a few days of intravenous nutrition, his color improved and his weight loss slowed. But his stomach rejected every attempt to deliver formula through the nasal tube. He vomited constantly and the diarrhea got worse; he cried and could not be soothed; his eyes told us he was in constant pain.

Andy's white blood cell count was even higher than it had been with the meningitis attack. After more tests, we learned an intractable new bug, *cytomegalovirus*, known as *CMV*, was eating away the lining of his colon, causing bleeding ulcers. Then he got a fungus infection, a known side effect of too many antibiotics, and another eye infection. Then he got pneumonia.

The weeks in the hospital turned into a month, then two, then three. Paulina had long ago stopped returning home at the end of each day. The two of us would bunk down in Andy's room for a sleepless night, and I'd go to work each morning almost blind with fatigue. Paulina broke down in tears nearly every day, sobbing, "I can't help him get better, I can't stop his pain, I can't even feed my own baby! What kind of mother does that make me?"

I tried to comfort her, but sometimes I'd feel a flash of unreasonable anger—how could she expect me to take care of her fears and doubts and depression as well as my own? Then would come a flood of shame. How had we come to this, so depleted we had nothing left for each other? I did my weeping alone in the hospital shower, but it brought no relief, only more fatigue. I needed all my strength for the endless task of figuring out what the doctors were saying, catching them in contradictions, forcing them to try something— anything—when they seemed to hit a wall. With each new setback, we had only Kretschmer to help figure out how to halt the cycle of infection, medication, side effect and more infection.

Reprieve

Two weeks before Christmas, the cycle broke. After three consecutive days without a fever, and a renewed tolerance for formula through the nasal tube, Andy was considered stable enough to go home. Besides that, we'd maxed out our insurance coverage. The hospital let us know we had overstayed our welcome by slipping the bill under our door early one morning, like a hotel. The total was more than I earned in a year. When I asked for an itemization, it took two hours to print out—every diaper was listed separately. My father, father-in-law and grandfather helped me pay the bill, and my dad quickly found a better insurance company for us, one that would accept treatment in the US. A higher premium, but worth it.

Paulina and I felt ready to care for Andy on our own. We learned how to re-thread the nasal tube that popped out every time he cried or coughed, and we knew how to schedule his seven daily medications. Paulina's joy at being home fueled a brief whirlwind of shopping and decorating. Our Christmas tree was a work of art, covered in handcrafted ornaments from Chiapas. We cautiously celebrated the holiday with a festive dinner, a bottle of cabernet and our baby in his portable seat on the dining room table. "Maybe I should put some wine in your feeding tube," I told Andy. Paulina chuckled and Andy joined in, happy to see us laughing. Friends and family stopped by on their way to various parties, but we were content to be housebound. Andy held court, sociable and bright-eyed with all the attention. His cheeks had regained some fullness and a few visitors remarked, "He looks fine! —how long does he need the nose tube?" They didn't notice that at 8 months old, Andy weighed only 10 pounds. His muscles were so underdeveloped he could no longer roll over, let alone sit unsupported. His fevers would come and go almost every day. He still had weekly appointments with Kretschmer and the gastroenterologist. We took him to the hospital every two weeks for immune-boosting gamma globulin infusions. Still, we allowed ourselves to relax a little, to find pleasure in familiar domestic routines and to feel optimistic about the coming new year.

The view from Andy's room at Hospital ABC.

Popocatepetl and Iztaccihuatl from Andy's window.

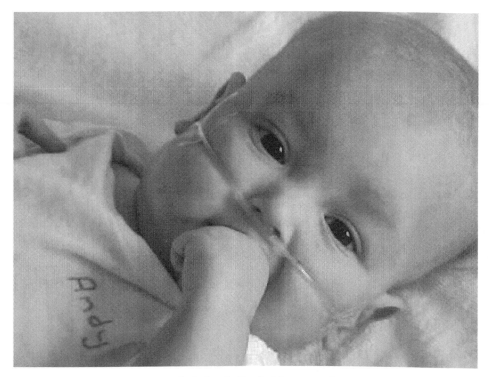

Andy hospitalized with pneumonia.

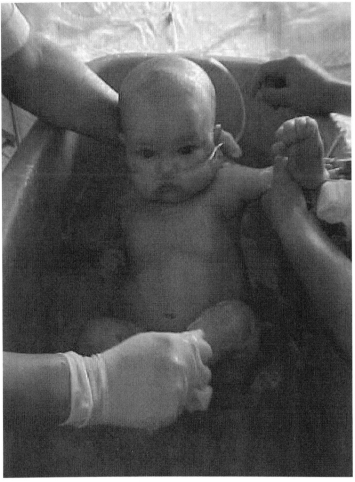

Nurses giving Andy a bath at Hospital ABC.

Andy's first Christmas, home at last.

Chapter Six
The Millennium

On December 31, 1999, while we were visiting my parents' Cuernavaca villa, Andy's fever shot up—he had a urinary tract infection. As a large Millennium Eve party swirled through the rest of the house, we huddled in a bedroom with another guest, a military doctor and old friend of my father's. He gave Andy an antibiotic injection. We were surrounded by music and laughter, but we were too distracted and worried to feel like celebrating the turn of the new century. Our only wish for the coming year was that our luck would change, that Andy would be diagnosed, that we'd find a cure for whatever was killing our son.

Denver

"I've made arrangements for you to take Andy to my old friend and colleague, Dr. Erwin Gelfand, at the National Jewish Hospital in Denver," Kretschmer announced at our next appointment. "He may repeat some of the immune tests I've done and offer some new ones I don't have access to. And I've also made an appointment with a gastroenterologist at Denver Children's Hospital."

Finally, we'd be trying the "option two" that Dr. Maulen had offered so many months ago—US medicine. One of Paulina's cousins, Marta, was living in Denver, and she and her husband invited us to stay with them while Andy was evaluated. With medical records transferred, visas secured and airline tickets purchased, we left for Denver on March 6, 2000. It turned out to be a longer stay than we'd planned.

Seeing a hospital totally devoted to pediatrics was a revelation. The Denver Children's parking lot was decorated with Disney characters, the halls and exam rooms were bright with artwork. The X-ray and MRI equipment were scaled down for small bodies. The nurses wore cartoon-printed scrubs and stethoscopes festooned with tiny toys— and they knew how to get an instant smile from Andy. In a place so devoted to kids and families, it was easier to feel hopeful.

Dr. Sokol, the gastroenterologist, was an energetic, outdoorsy-looking guy in his early 40s. He interviewed us in an empty playroom where we sat with our knees jackknifed on tiny chairs at a child-sized table. Shy about her English, Paulina remained silent while I spent 45 minutes recounting Andy's medical history. Dr. Sokol kept raising his eyebrows and peering at the baby sitting in his stroller next to us. "You've got a miracle boy here. Lucky to be alive."

He wanted another endoscopy right away, so we brought Andy to the radiology department. We held hands in the waiting room, Paulina whispering, "Dear God, please help Andy get well. Please let this be the place where he gets well."

But when we got the results I felt a familiar sensation, a clamp on my chest screwing down tight. Paulina's face told me she felt it, too. None of the treatments of the last 10 months had worked. The ulcers in Andy's colon were back, as well as new ulcers on his esophagus from the feeding tube. Dr. Sokol suspected the biopsies he took might show more *cytomegalovirus*. He arranged to have copies of the results sent over to Dr. Gelfand, the chief of Immunology at the National Jewish Hospital nearby, where our next appointment was scheduled.

The next day, Andy had a complete immunology evaluation with the portly and affable Dr. Gelfand, who'd been a medical fellow at Children's Hospital Boston with Kretschmer in the 60s. "My friend Roberto has done a very thorough job with your son," he told us as he took blood samples from Andy. "We'll repeat the tests here, but there's not much more testing we can offer. In the meantime, Dr. Sokol can take the lead treating Andy's diarrhea and malnutrition—maybe if those conditions improve, his immune response will get better also. Let's set another appointment for tomorrow to complete the blood draws."

But we never got to that second appointment. The next day, the endoscopy biopsy confirmed the *cytomegalovirus* was definitely back and Andy needed to be admitted to Denver Children's for a course of antivirals. Dr. Sokol wanted to treat Andy's inflamed colon with a more powerful antacid, try a different feeding formula and add intravenous nutrition at night to maximize weight gain. In a bizarre complication, overnight Andy's index finger had swollen to twice the normal size. Sokol immediately ordered a bone scan. It showed Andy had osteomyelitis, a bone infection, and it would require four weeks of antibiotics. The infectious disease specialist told us that bacteria roaming around in Andy's blood found its way to the bone in his finger. The news of yet another invading bug was terrifying—what if bacteria attacked his heart or another organ? Why was this happening?

Once again we were hospital prisoners, our faith in a magical American treatment slipping away. We slept only a few hours a night. I was anxious about mounting medical costs and worried about being away from my job for so long, even though my brother, who was running the family company from Mexico City now, was great at figuring out ways for me to telecommute. My head ached from trying to understand a different medical culture. We were already accustomed to repeating everything doctors said to us—now that we were dealing in English I continued even more slowly and carefully. Paulina let me be the one to puzzle things out.

"Don't tell me everything they're saying—just condense it for me. It's too much information and it only confuses me more." She'd narrowed her concerns to the confines of Andy's crib, to keeping him comforted, reassured and distracted. And I agreed. Andy needed the extraordinary level of attention only his mother could give.

Andy submitted to more tests. Because long-term parenteral nutrition is known to damage kidneys and liver, he went in for an abdominal ultrasound, which came back normal. Then he had an eye exam to make sure the *cytomegalovirus* hadn't attacked his retina—it was also normal. The tiny vein in his arm would no longer take an intravenous needle, so he had one inserted in his scalp, tied to his head with a gauze cap. He looked like a cute alien. Eventually the doctors decided to abandon the intravenous tubes and insert a catheter directly in his chest. After each procedure, Andy woke from the blessing of anesthesia and managed to give us a big smile, holding out his arms. I was grateful that for a few hours at least, he was pain free.

Dr. Gelfand sent a hematologist over to take another leukocyte function test. A week later the hematologist told us, "The test came back negative, so I have no explanation for your son's elevated white blood cell count. Maybe he has his own syndrome."

And as the other immune test results came in, Dr. Gelfand confirmed, "Nothing unusual has shown up. His functions are normal—I can't find evidence of an immune deficiency, even though all his symptoms would indicate that. If you can get his stomach problems under control, his overall condition may improve." I couldn't tell if that was good news or bad. Gelfand wished us luck, and sent his report back to Kretschmer.

After 10 inpatient days, Andy's finger was better, his gut had recovered and he gained one-and-half pounds on the new formula. Dr. Sokol discharged us with instructions to continue the intravenous antibiotic and antiviral treatment through Andy's catheter for at least another 14 days. Our insurance covered a home health care consult to show us how to handle the catheter and infuse medications "at home." But we had no home here, and returning to Mexico in the middle of treatment made no sense.

After one night back at Paulina's cousin's place, when Andy woke crying four times and we spilled medication that left an indelible orange stain on the carpet, Paulina said, "We can't impose on them for another two or three weeks, it's just too much!"

I knew she was right. My parents came to the rescue, sending us enough customer reward points to check us into a suite at the local Marriott Residence Inn. The home health care company set us up with inventory: medicines and formula in the mini-fridge; tubes, syringes and disposable gloves stacked on the coffee table; a pole next to the portable crib to carry the intravenous infusion pumps.

In the meantime, I was desperate to return to work—I'd exhausted the possibilities of off-site productivity for a while. But I couldn't leave Paulina and Andy alone. My mother arrived for a weekend to help out, and when she left, another one of Paulina's cousins, Alejandra, flew in. As soon as Paulina felt comfortable handling things without me, I returned to Mexico City.

It was the first time since Andy's birth we'd been separated for more than a matter of hours, and I hated it. Paulina called with updates every night, but it was an endless three weeks before I returned to Denver. When I entered our room at the Marriott, Paulina handed the baby to Alejandra and stepped into my arms in a long, silent hug. She was pale, with dark shadows under her eyes, but she tilted her chin up and smiled the way I loved. Andy looked stronger and chubby-cheeked—he was up to 17 pounds—and he squealed on Ale's lap when he saw me.

The next day, at our follow-up appointment, Dr. Sokol told us Andy seemed strong enough to travel, and we could return to Mexico and continue the antivirals orally. Paulina was reluctant to leave Denver, fearful of re-entering our old vicious cycle in Mexican hospitals. But we'd run out of Marriott points and reached our insurance policy's limit for US treatment. Sokol agreed to stay in touch with Dr. Madrazo, our Mexican gastroenterologist, and we agreed to keep Andy on the new formula, Neocate. Since the manufacturer had no Mexican distributor, I knew I'd be calling the Monterrey smuggler again. On April 22, we headed for home, our luggage full of Neocate boxes and our hearts full of doubt.

Sliding Backwards

Within two days of our return, we discovered red oozing spots on Andy's legs—a skin infection that sent us back to Hospital ABC. Another round of gut-destroying antibiotics led, predictably, to diarrhea, feeding problems and a fresh opportunity for a *cytomegalovirus* invasion. Between his stomach pain and a new discomfort—teething—Andy cried nearly constantly and couldn't be comforted. He began regularly vomiting the Neocate formula we'd counted on to help him build strength to fight infection. Dr. Madrazo put Andy back on the old formula, with no improvement. We watched helplessly as the baby lost weight again—at 12 pounds he was nearing the bottom of the growth chart for 11-month-olds. After another endoscopy showed the esophagus ulcers worsening, our old friend Dr. Martínez-Natera removed the nasal feeding tube and gave Andy a new central line to receive parenteral nutrition while his stomach had a prolonged rest. It was as though the Denver advances had never happened.

We got through the next few weeks at Hospital ABC on a depressingly familiar track. It was hard to be greeted by all the nurses and our favorite cleaning lady with—"Oh no, you're back again?" But their friendship and kindness sustained us, and my parents visited every day.

By May 2, our third wedding anniversary, the antibiotics and antivirals were finished and Martínez-Natera surprised us by suggesting Andy be released to home care, as long as Kretschmer and Madrazo agreed. "It's the first time we've ever allowed a pediatric patient to get TPN outside the hospital," he said, "but I really think a home environment will be good for your son."

"Well, he's certainly not doing very well here in the hospital," Paulina said. "Why do you think he'll do better at home?"

"It will be less stressful for him—and for you. I do think he'll get better eventually, but I don't know to what degree."

"But why? Why is it taking so long?" she persisted.

Martínez-Natera looked uncomfortable—he was another one who liked having the right answers. "Maybe your son has a new type of disease, one that hasn't been named yet. We can't treat what we can't define," he replied in his brusque way. "Now, I know you already have some experience, but I'll teach you how to manage his catheter, change his dressing, connect the nutrition bags and use the infusion pump. You'll also need a home nurse—I'll give her some training myself."

"I think they're sending us home because they just can't do anything else for Andy," Paulina said to me later. And our insurance company was resisting paying for this latest hospitalization, claiming it was for a "pre-existing condition."

First birthday

We got home on May 14, the day before Andy's first birthday. We managed to celebrate on the 15th with a few family members, surrounded by so much hospital equipment our apartment might have been the pediatric ward. Andy was too weak to respond to his guests with much more than a smile. He was showing his first two teeth, but it surprised us that they were upper teeth, instead of the lower ones we'd seen on so many other babies. Plus, they were pointed, like a baby shark's. We made a note to ask Kretschmer. Maybe it was another side effect of antibiotics.

Paulina was soon competent in handing all of Andy's procedures with Esther, the home nurse. But Andy lost his central line again, and Dr. Martínez-Natera sent us to a catheter specialist. Dr. Melgoza was a straight-talking military surgeon, who told us he'd trained in the States, in Pittsburgh. I liked him. "How many caths has this little man had?" he asked.

"Six, I think you can count all the different scars…" I answered.

"Well, let's try something different," Melgoza said. He showed us a double-tubed catheter, called a Broviac, which is inserted directly into the chest and can accommodate two tubes for multiple infusions. "Two ports, this is exactly what you need, little man," he told Andy. "Better and easier."

"Oh, my poor baby," said Paulina when Andy came out of the operating room, groggy, with the new double tube sprouting from his chest. "How will we ever explain all these holes and scars to you when you're older? Let's go home."

At home, on a disciplined daily schedule, Paulina flushed his central line and kept his new catheter site clean. She administered medications and tested his blood and urine for sugar and electrolyte levels. She managed the intravenous nutrition bags and 24-hour intravenous infusion pumps. Even with help from Esther, the home care nurse, it was a long, grueling day, and Paulina never faltered. I was terrified to touch the equipment, convinced I'd break or contaminate something. Not for the first time, I was in awe of my wife.

For my part, I came home from the office each evening and entered Andy's daily meds, tube feedings and blood chemistry readings on an Excel spreadsheet. I spent hours on insurance reimbursement forms, battling the insurance company over coverage and their definition of "pre-existing condition" and "individual hospitalization events." And I tried to entertain my son as he lay tethered by cables to his crib or stroller, like a little Gulliver. He endured the discomforts of the intravenous tubes, the meds, and the pump as though this was normal life. When he wasn't violently sick or in pain, he'd babble conversationally and call out to us, reaching up his arms to be held. His favorite toys were empty tubes and oral syringes. His smile whenever we soothed him or played with him was all we needed to keep going, even if we weren't sure of our direction.

But Paulina's endurance had its limits. One afternoon I came home to pick her up for a meeting with our health insurance representative at my office. Esther had taken Andy in his stroller down into the garden. I found my wife making arrangements to take Andy to one of the local public hospitals, where insurance wasn't required.

"I have to complete these public assistance forms," she said to me. "I was talking with my cousin and she suggested that since we're not getting anywhere with any other doctors …" She stopped when she saw the look on my face.

"Are you crazy?!! Those hospitals are terrible! Andy would have died of infection or neglect months ago in a place like that! How could you even think of such a bad idea?" I shouted.

Paulina's face contorted with grief and anger. "You don't know how I feel!" she cried. "You have no idea what it's like to be a mother and not be able to feed my baby! Every day, I watch him suffer! I can't take it anymore!" Her voice rose, "And you don't help me! All you do is ask me if I've fed him, and how much I've fed him! Who do you think is measuring the formula and trying to get him to eat? You don't know how it feels to be struggling with him every damn minute of every damn day, day in and day out!"

My own anger exploded. "That's bullshit! Of course I know how you feel—do you think it's any easier for me, his father? I can't stand seeing him suffer either, but that's no reason for us to make a stupid decision! Taking him to a government hospital will only be a dangerous waste of time. There are so many other things we can try! You're being ridiculous!!"

I was losing it—I grabbed my car keys and headed out the door before I said anything more. I could hear Paulina's deep, wrenching sobs behind me as I pounded down the stairs.

Her email reached me a few hours later at my office.

> *"Mi Amor, perdóname. I'm hurting so badly and I just want it to stop. I should have thought this through more clearly—I just wanted another option, another cushion to fall back on. I'm Andy's mother, I'm desperate to help him—I'd move heaven and earth for him, but I don't know how. Please forgive what I said. I couldn't have chosen a better father for my son. You've been incredible through all this. You and Andy are my whole world. I love you very much. I'm at home, waiting for you."*

It wasn't hard to email back:

> *"Paulina, I'm hurting too. And the worst of it is, we're not acting as a team. We can discuss anything you want, but emotional outbursts aren't going to get us anywhere. There are other, positive steps we can take for our insurance and financial problems—like more careful budgeting, getting updated on reimbursements, looking for a better insurance plan. But besides that, we need to remember that the doctors are not infallible—as we've seen. The one with ultimate responsibility for Andy is God. Next are you and I. We made the decision to have a baby, and we make the decisions for his care. Together. And thanks to you, he's out of the hospital and doing better than he was. Let's take better care of each other. Let's focus on what's most important for Andy, and try not to get mired in the daily ordeal. It goes without saying that you and Andy are everything to me. Let's move forward."*

Then I went home.

Crisis

With Andy's 24/7 care, our sleep was reduced to a few hours a day. In addition to Esther's daytime help, we hired a private nurse to stay overnight with the baby several times a week so we could have an occasional uninterrupted rest. Early on the morning of July 15, the overnight nurse woke us with the news that Andy had been crying and fussing all night unless he was being wheeled back and forth in his stroller.

After the nurse left, Paulina scooped Andy up, crooning, "Who gave his nurse a hard time last night?" He dropped his pacifier and when she picked it up, she cried out, "Aihh! Andrés! There's blood on Andy's pacifier!"

I immediately called Dr. Kretschmer. "Give him a strong liquid antacid," he ordered. "Bring him in and I'll take a look at him."

Paulina ran down to the corner pharmacy for the antacid, while I held Andy in the rocking chair, thinking the rhythm would calm him. But he started screaming and arching his back. "*¿Qué pasó, Andy?* What is it? Shh, shh."

Nothing I did soothed him, he screeched and kicked. His stomach seemed taut as a drum. *Where's Paulina?* His head felt hot. *Why is Paulina taking so long?* Andy coughed and gagged, then vomited blood all over my arm. I was starting to panic, but I heard Paulina at the door so I yelled, "*¡Vámonos al hospital! ¡Vámonos!*- We're going to the hospital! Now! Let's go, let's go!"

Paulina struggled to hold Andy in the back seat while I drove like a maniac to Hospital ABC. Dodging traffic and praying, I speed-dialed Dr. Vazquez's number. She met us in the emergency room and hustled us into an exam room. Andy was thrashing—we'd never seen him in such agony. The pediatric surgeon, Dr. Torres, immediately vented the gas buildup in Andy's stomach through a tube down his throat. "Could be an intestinal occlusion," he said. "If it's a twist or blockage, we may have to cut out the affected tissue and reconnect the intestine. It could also be appendicitis, but that's unheard of in a child this young." I could barely process this news.

"How can he have a blockage when he doesn't eat anything?" I asked.

"We definitely have to open him up and have a look, and we need to act now," Dr. Torres answered. "I'm going to prep for surgery. Meet me at the OR on the first floor."

I'd called my parents, and as soon as they arrived they accompanied us down to the operating room. I carried Andy gently into the elevator, trying not to bump his tender abdomen. He was moaning, but calmer, and Paulina held his hand, murmuring. A nurse wearing blue scrubs and a mask took Andy from me in the OR hallway. With effort, he twisted away from her and held out his arms, calling to us, his eyes pleading. My voice cracked as I called out, "You take good care of him!" Then the operating room door closed.

I gripped Paulina's arm as we returned to the pediatric unit. The next four hours were the worst of my life. I couldn't respond to my parents' simplest comments, I couldn't pray and couldn't quell my frantic thoughts. Remove part of his intestine? How could Andy's beleaguered little body withstand that major trauma? How would he ever be able to eat normally now? I was on the edge of losing control. Paulina sat murmuring prayers and fingering her rosary as each minute crawled by.

Finally, the phone rang. *"Señor Treviño?* Your son is doing fine—he's in the recovery room. It was appendicitis, and it hadn't ruptured yet—just an infection. I removed it."

Paulina slumped with relief, so I hung up and just held her as my parents embraced both of us.

When I called to let Kretschmer know, he said, "Appendicitis? In a 14-month old? That's the first case I've ever heard of. Tell Torres to save the appendix tissue for me—I want to examine it in my lab."

Dr. Torres had said, "Given all the other possibilities, appendicitis is very good news." It was hard to accept another infection, and such an abnormal one as well. *Everything* was abnormal about our case.

I tried to believe that things couldn't get any worse; that this would be the beginning of a turnaround. And I never wanted to return to the mental hell I'd just experienced. I vowed I'd keep a firmer grip on my mind and emotions. For Andy's sake, I had to stay positive.

Losing options

While the appendicitis incision was healing, Dr. Torres tried to convince us to let him implant a feeding tube directly into Andy's stomach. The ever-present risk of liver damage from the intravenous nutrition scared us, but a gastrostomy—making a hole in Andy's torso to insert a tube— sounded so ghastly we decided to attempt oral feeding again.

In the following days we tried everything. Bottles, nipples, cups, syringes, spoons and tubes. With background music, without. Lights on, or dim. In his crib, on the sofa, in the hospital hallways. He just cried and turned away from whatever we held to his lips. We constantly asked Dr. Madrazo for feeding tips. Nothing worked. Andy wouldn't eat and couldn't gain weight.

Then Andy lost his fancy new Broviac double catheter. The tip popped out of his heart and his intravenous formula seeped into his chest and shoulder—it looked puffy and painful. "Have you decided about the G-tube yet?" asked Dr. Torres, prepping Andy for the catheter reinsertion. He wanted to take advantage of the anesthesia and do the tube procedure at the same time. "I really think it would improve things. He'll still get intravenous nutrition as a supplement for a while, but you can also keep trying oral feeding, which you can't do with the naso-gastric tube. Plus that tube gave him esophageal ulcers."

"How can I consent to this—another hole in him?" Paulina asked, turning to me.

"But if this will enable him to get stronger without liver damage, and maybe start eating again, we should do it," I answered. We agreed to go ahead. After the operation, I had to coax Paulina to look at his G-tube, but it wasn't so bad. We were used to seeing tubes and catheters inserted in our son—this was just bigger.

Now it was mid-August, and we were missing out on another summer. But the bougainvillea was blooming on our apartment balcony, and we were just happy to go home. Of course, Paulina became expert at taking care of the stomach tube. We had weekly appointments with Dr. Madrazo to lower the nutrition through his veins and increase the tube feeds.

Within weeks, Andy's central line popped out again.

This time, Dr. Melgoza, the catheter specialist, met us in the hallway outside his office. He said with a lowered voice, "Listen, and don't tell anyone what I'm about to say." Looking over his shoulder, he continued, "I'm telling you as a friend, not as your surgeon. Your doctors here have run out of ideas on how to treat your son. They've used all the resources available in Mexico; there are no more options. Go to the United States—it's your only hope for getting a diagnosis."

"No more options?" I didn't like the way that sounded.

"Don't get me wrong—I'm happy to change catheters daily if it comes to that," Melgoza said. "But we're not getting anywhere."

We knew he was right. And we also knew where we'd probably go.

On Kretschmer's advice, Andy had started physical therapy with Maria, a woman who lived next door to our apartment building. At 15 months, he was still so weak he could barely sit up. He loved the sessions with his therapist— he thought it was play. Paulina reported that when Maria learned Andy's story, she kept talking about her cousin, a pediatric gastroenterologist in the States. "His name is Samuel Nurko—he's at Children's Hospital in Boston. Maybe he could help you." Now we were ready to use the phone numbers she'd given Paulina.

Naturally, first I turned to Kretschmer. After all, he'd studied and worked at the same Boston hospital, where his friend and colleague Dr. Raif Geha was now chief of immunology. Kretschmer didn't hesitate.

"Going to Children's Hospital Boston? Sounds like a good idea," he rumbled. "I remember meeting Nurko, you'll be in good hands. Call me when you find Geha. And good luck."

Paulina and I mobilized. Andy got a temporary fix for his catheter, though the site was still red and swollen. I bought airline tickets for the first flight I could find to Boston, which had a plane change in Chicago. I got extra intravenous nutrition bags for when we arrived, but during the flight Andy would be without the intravenous tubes and pumps and wouldn't be getting any real nutrition. Dr. Madrazo showed us how to give Andy concentrated electrolyte gel directly through his G-tube, to keep his blood sugar stable during the long trip. I knew it was risky. We'd have only a 12-hour window before Andy had to be hooked up again.

On Sunday September 10, 2000, I called Dr. Nurko's home phone number, explained who I was and told him Andy's story. He listened courteously, and then told me we were rushing things. "It's not a good idea to travel if you have to interrupt the intravenous nutrition," he cautioned. "Sounds like your son isn't well enough to make the trip yet. Besides, we need a few weeks to get the proper referrals and make appointments here."

"Dr. Nurko, we don't have weeks," I answered. "His catheter is failing. We're arriving tomorrow evening, and we'll go directly to your emergency room."

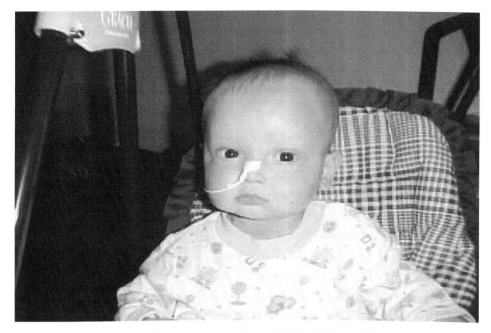

Andy with a naso-gastric tube at Children's Hospital Denver.

PART TWO

THE DIAGNOSIS HUNT

Chapter Seven
Boston

"Children's Hospital, 300 Longwood Avenue," I told the cab driver at Logan Airport. He took one look at Andy's tubes and pumps and drove as if he couldn't wait to get rid of us. We emerged from a long tunnel into late evening, Boston's twisting streets speeding by.

Stepping into Children's Hospital was like disembarking on a new planet. The lobby was empty and calm, with a tropical fish tank, colorful murals and a huge kinetic sculpture. Standing there with two overnight bags, a stroller and a desperately sick baby, I felt painfully disoriented. Paulina's face was gray with exhaustion and I knew I looked rumpled and unshaven. We'd spent the 12-hour flight and layover trying to cool Andy's fever, clean his catheter, administer his medications and clean up the constant vomiting and diarrhea. We'd ignored the appalled glances of fellow passengers.

In the ER, the admitting nurse greeted us warmly and gave us a note from Dr. Nurko—he'd already left for the day but he'd be meeting with us the next morning. My heart lifted. Despite the short notice, they were welcoming us.

An Emergency Department resident interviewed us, recording Andy's medical history for more than an hour. Then he called in an infectious disease specialist to look at the oozing catheter site in Andy's chest. "Smells like an *enterococcus* infection—we'll run a test," the specialist said. "We may have to pull out the central line. In the meantime, he'll need 10 days of intravenous antibiotics." The old routine.

We took the elevator up to the general medical ward on the eighth floor, where a pretty young nurse with dark curly hair smiled and beckoned to us. Ana Maria spoke some Spanish, but we understood her better in English. We watched in astonishment as she set up a cornucopia of diapers and supplies in our room—more than we'd ever seen at one time in any Mexican hospital. Andy was whimpering from all the strangeness, and I held him as Paulina started to put clean sheets on the crib. Ana Maria gently stopped her, made up the crib and took Andy from my arms.

"I can see what a tough job you've had, Mom and Dad," she said. "You just relax now, I'll take care of getting him comfortable."

Paulina stood close by, watching the baby for signs of distress. Andy eyed Ana Maria warily as she changed his diaper and chattered in a mix of Spanish and English.

"*Mira*, let's put on these nice pajamas, *sí*?" She never winced when she saw his swollen abdomen, bristling with intravenous ports and catheters. "Now, *that* looks very uncomfortable," she commented on his stomach tube. "You need a mic-key button, cutie-pie." She glanced at us, "That's a newer kind of feeding tube with a little implanted button. It's flat to the skin, instead of this clunky connector."

She deftly cleaned around Andy's central line and secured it to his t-shirt with white tape and a diaper pin. We were agape—if only someone had shown us how to do that six months ago, Andy wouldn't have accidentally pulled out his catheter so many times.

By 10 p.m., the baby finally slept, and Paulina collapsed on the green sofa next to his crib. "Things are different here, but in a good way," she said, yawning. "They seem to know what they're doing."

"Get some sleep." I kissed her and wandered down the hall to a lounge, pushed several chairs together, and passed out for a few hours, too.

The right place

Early the next morning, a smiling, mustached man in blue scrubs and a white lab coat entered our room, accompanied by two interns. *"Hola, ¡Buenos días! Yo soy Sam Nurko,"* he said, extending both hands. We gripped them like drowning swimmers. Paulina thanked him effusively for last night's note in the emergency room. Dr. Nurko turned to the baby. Andy stared at the thick mustache and smiled tentatively when Dr. Nurko greeted him in Spanish.

As the interns leaned against the wall and Dr. Nurko settled with us on the couch, I related—in English, for the interns' benefit—Andy's 16-month medical history. The blood infection at birth. The *E. coli* infection in his gut. The meningitis, pneumonia, strep infections, eye infections, skin infections, urinary tract infections, osteomyelitis and appendicitis. The recurrent ulcerative colitis, the feeding intolerance, the intravenous nutrition and the G-tube. The cone-shaped teeth. The failure to grow.

"And every immune function test has come back negative; even the ones we took him to Denver for were inconclusive. We've run out of options in Mexico. The doctors we most respect all told us to go to Boston," I said.

"You've come to the right place," Dr. Nurko answered. "We'll do a full gastrointestinal work up once the catheter infection is better. I recommend pulling out the cath and also trying a new feeding formula through his gastrostomy. You'll be here for at least 10 days for those antibiotics, but I'll take some GI X-rays in the meantime. I'm also ordering hematology and immunology consults while you're here."

"He said we've done the right thing, coming here," Paulina said after he left. At the look of hope on her beautiful, tired face I felt an echoing surge that made my chest ache.

After 10 days, the central line infection cleared. Andy was tolerating his new formula, and Dr. Nurko replaced Andy's stomach tube with a tidy mickey button. Then Nurko began his investigation, first with X-rays, then an endoscopy.

The radiology department was decorated with big posters of x-rayed toys —Mr. Potato Head, Barbie, a fire truck. "Look, we're going to take some pictures of your stomach, Andy," I told him. He gave his best "say cheese!" smile. For the endoscopy, they gave him a "happy drug" before the anesthesia, so he wouldn't remember going into the OR without us. I knew what Paulina was thinking: how much trauma could have been avoided when Andy was repeatedly taken from our arms, screaming, if only they'd had "happy drugs" in Mexico.

Two hours later, his face sober, Dr. Nurko showed us the images of multiple ulcers deep in Andy's intestines. Paulina sucked in her breath, "Ooh, that must hurt!"

"Do you think this might be what he's had before, when the *CMV* attacked his gut?" I asked. "Our Mexican doctors wanted to try steroids—do you think we should do that? Should I have the previous slides sent here for comparison?"

"Good idea to get the slides," he nodded. "I took biopsies, and we'll have results in 48 hours. When we're sure it's *cytomegalovirus* we can decide whether to use steroids. It's more of a last resort. And don't worry about his pain. We can give him the medication for that."

On Wednesday, Dr. Nurko came around with results. The *cytomegalovirus* was still wreaking havoc in Andy's intestines, and it meant another antiviral regimen. Meanwhile, pain meds and the vigilance of Paulina and the nurses were keeping Andy relatively comfortable. He was getting used to this hospital. He was secure in our undivided attention every waking moment. He also liked flirting with Ana Maria and reaching for Nurko's mustache. His favorite plaything was the yellow measuring tape used to gauge his belly's circumference. He called it his "aii" and he'd handle it for hours, saying "aaiii, aaiiii," to himself.

Chapter Eight
Gathering Clues

One morning, soon after the *cytomegalovirus* infection was confirmed, an athletically-built man with a stethoscope and a chart stood in the door of Andy's room. He had a smooth, young face and was wearing a purple shirt and lavender tie, no lab coat. He held out his hand, "Hello, Mr. Treviño, I'm Dr. Jordan Orange. I'm an immunology post-doc here. Do you mind if I examine your son?"

This guy didn't look much older than I, but his hospital ID badge had an MD and a PhD after his name. A physician/scientist.

"Please come in." I shook his hand. "Immunology. You must know Dr. Raif Geha. Our Mexican immunologist, Roberto Kretschmer, used to work with him."

"Yes, of course, Dr. Geha is our chief immunologist. I gather you've also met Dr. Gelfand from the National Jewish Hospital in Denver; he used to work here, too. You've had a very extensive immune workup."

"Well, yes, and all the tests seem to come back negative." I told him.

"But I think there's one test missing," Dr. Orange continued. "My PhD thesis was on natural killer cells. Are you familiar with immune system terminology?"

"Somewhat familiar," I answered. "Dr. Kretschmer used to coach me whenever Andy had a new test. I remember him telling me that natural killer cells are the immune system's first line of defense—they directly kill certain tumors and viruses without needing other signals or any help from other parts of the immune system."

"That's correct. Your son's medical chart shows he's especially vulnerable to the *CMV*, which natural killer cells usually attack right away," he said. "If you allow me, I'd like to study your son's NK cell function."

His calm confidence made me instantly comfortable, but Paulina eyed him suspiciously.

"Tell him thank you, but we really don't need more immune tests," she said to me in Spanish. "The doctors in Mexico and Denver told us to fix the stomach problems and then maybe his immune response will get better. Dr. Nurko is working on Andy's stomach infections now." She turned back to Andy.

I gestured to Dr. Orange and we walked out into the hall. "Tell me more."

"We need more information about your son's natural killer cell deficits, especially since it could explain the connection to specific infections like *cytomegalovirus*," he said. "We'll also need a blood sample from his mother. In other words, we'll check to see if Andy's NK cells are able to fight *cytomegalovirus* and we'll use your wife's sample as a control."

"Sounds good to me. It would be great if you could talk to Dr. Kretschmer in Mexico and see what other results he might already have," I said.

"Let's do it now," he said.

Ignoring Paulina's frown, I dialed Roberto Kretschmer in Mexico City and put the call on speakerphone. In his booming voice, Kretschmer gave a full recitation of all Andy's immunology tests in Denver and Mexico, from memory. Dr. Orange listened attentively, and then said, "Well, *that* was valuable. But I think there's more we can do."

He turned to Andy and greeted him so sweetly the baby gave him a huge grin. Reluctantly, Paulina nodded her consent, and Dr. Orange took a blood sample from each of them. Two days later he gave us the results:

DEFICIENT NK KILLING FUNCTION IN BOTH MOTHER AND PATIENT.

Finally a test showed something definitively wrong with Andy's defenses! We were excited—but also puzzled.

"How could my function also be deficient? I'm healthy!" said Paulina.

Dr. Orange answered thoughtfully. "There's still so much we don't know about how all the immune components work together, and that's why tests can reveal only part of the big picture. Even if Paulina's NK function is compromised, the rest of her system may be normal enough to compensate. Andy's system *isn't* compensating, so there's much more about his function we need to explore."

"If we can now pinpoint this killer cell problem, could there be a cure?" I asked Dr. Orange.

His answer was cautious. "I think my lab here can come up with some new treatment directions to follow—but it will take a little time."

Dr. Orange prescribed immune-boosting gamma globulin infusions for Andy, the same medication we'd occasionally used in Mexico. For the next week or so he stopped by almost every day to play with Andy and try to make him laugh. His friendliness was contagious as he told us about his wife, Katie, and 6-month-old daughter, Audrey, and asked about our lives in Mexico. Paulina soon welcomed his visits as much as I did—*"¡Mira, Andy, aquí está Dr. Orange!* Look, here's Dr. Orange!"* she'd say, lifting the baby to greet him. We missed our families and friends, but Jordan Orange helped alleviate the boredom of being trapped in a hospital room day and night.

As soon as Andy's central line infection cleared, we were free to go home. Dr. Nurko discharged us with a medication regimen, new feeding formula and an appointment for follow-up in a month. Stressful as it was to take care of Andy without round-the-clock nursing help, Paulina couldn't wait to re-enter our life in Mexico. Real food! Our own bathroom! Our own bed! But I had mixed feelings about leaving the place where answers seemed just around the corner.

Second clue: no sweat

In four weeks, we returned to Boston for follow-up. Andy still had diarrhea, still couldn't gain weight, and had a strange patch of dry, scaly skin on his scalp that concerned Paulina, especially since his hair remained as thin as a newborn's.

We arrived back at Children's on Halloween and it appeared we were the only people in the entire hospital without a costume. The two nurses who prepped Andy for his colonoscopy were dressed as a devil and a rabbit. They were so entertaining Andy forgot to be afraid of the OR. As they wheeled his crib into the treatment room I watched their backs—one sporting a bunny puff, the other a snaky red tail.

The colonoscopy results were discouraging. Paulina's face was tense as Dr. Nurko pointed out many large and small lesions in Andy's lower intestine. "It's ulcerative colitis again. In addition to the *cytomegalovirus*, I think he has a second infection, maybe a return of the *clostridium difficile*," he said. "We need him admitted while we confirm this and start him on more antibiotics. And let's have a dermatologist check out that dry patch on his head."

This time we were sequestered in a private room—Andy was on "contact precautions" for a few days until the *C. difficile* was confirmed. He couldn't leave, not even for a trip down the hall in his stroller. His new nurse wore a bright yellow gown, gloves and face mask over which she'd attached a plastic pig-nose. Andy gave her one look and burst into tears until our old friend Ana Maria appeared in the doorway. She waved hello to him, but couldn't enter the room. "It's like being in a cage at the zoo," said Paulina. She bedded down on the couch, and I piled a few blankets and pillows on the floor.

At 7:00 the following morning, I struggled to stand up as five masked and gowned doctors entered the room and switched on the lights. Andy immediately started to cry; Paulina rubbed her eyes and reached for him. We were a family of extraterrestrials, about to be observed by a yellow-uniformed contamination squad.

"Good morning, sorry to wake you, we're from the Dermatology Department. We're here to examine your son," said the leader as the others watched him carefully. He reached under his gown and fished a magnifying lens out of his pocket. Above his mask, his gray eyebrows knitted together as he peered at Andy's scalp, hair, skin, and finally, his teeth. Andy lay quietly in Paulina's arms.

"Hmmm. Sparse hair, no sweat glands, pointy teeth. He has ectodermal dysplasia." And he swept from the room, followed by his entourage.

Paulina and I looked at each other. "What? What did he say?"

I hurried out the door after them, still in the sweatpants and T-shirt I slept in. One of the doctors turned back, his mask now dangling from his neck. His ID badge read *Paul Lerou, MD*. He must have been a resident—he looked about my age, and spoke in a deferential tone.

"That was Dr. Gellis, the Dermatology chief. He thinks your son has ectodermal dysplasia."

"Ecto...could you please write that down for me?" I asked, ducking back into the room for a pad.

Dr. Lerou addressed Paulina politely. "Good morning, Mrs. Treviño. May I ask you, does your son sweat?"

"Umm, no. I guess I've never seen him sweat, even though he has constant fevers. He feels hot, but dry."

"And do you sweat?" he asked her.

"Umm, yeah, I do. Not much, but I do sweat."

"I sweat a lot," I offered. "Why do you want to know?"

"We'll be back soon with more details, after we finish rounds. Dr. Gellis will explain everything then," he said, smiling. Then he continued down the hall.

When the team returned, Paulina and I strained to follow Dr. Gellis' explanation. "My head hurts," said Paulina afterwards.

I grabbed my laptop, Googled "ectodermal dysplasia" and found the website of the National Foundation for Ectodermal Dysplasia. I read aloud to Paulina, "The ectodermal syndromes are a large group of about 150 heritable disorders that affect the ectoderm, the outer layer of tissue in a developing fetus. The ectoderm contributes to the formation of many parts of the body, including skin, sweat glands, hair, teeth and nails. During embryonic development these and other parts of the body, including eyes, ears, nerves, fingers and toes, may fail to develop normally. Although in rare cases ectodermal dysplasia can affect lifespan, typically that is not the case." The website was full of photos of kids with cute faces, small noses, thin hair and few teeth. They looked a little like Andy. I glanced over at him. Another puzzle piece seemed to be falling into place.

"So…could this syndrome have anything to do with infections and ulcers and colitis?" Paulina voiced my next thoughts. "Or the NK cell study?"

The website listed a Mary Kaye Richter as the Foundation's director. I immediately emailed her, asking if she had any information about the possible relationship between ectodermal dysplasia and immune deficiency.

Paulina was fascinated by the website's information on the many types of ectodermal dysplasia syndromes, and by the countless stories of affected kids and their families. "Maybe these people can help us," she said, looking more animated than I'd seen her in months. She turned to Andy in his crib, "We're going to find out how to make you better, baby."

A doctor we'd never met before entered the room, introduced himself as a geneticist, and told us he needed a DNA sample to add more information to the ectodermal dysplasia diagnosis. He swabbed the inside of Andy's cheek with a tiny brush to collect skin cells, and packaged the swab to send to a Maryland genetics lab. "We'll have the results in three to four weeks—it will tell us whether he has some of the gene mutations associated with ectodermal dysplasia."

When Jordan Orange visited later, we couldn't wait to tell him about the new diagnosis. His eyes lit up. "If it's a genetic mutation, there could very well be a connection to the NK deficiency," he said. "While you're waiting for the gene test, I'd like to get another blood sample and see if I can grow Andy's immune cells in my lab. A cell line will help us continue to study that NK function."

I was both excited and frustrated. "Grow a cell line? How long are we talking about? I can't afford to be here much longer—we're running out of money. What are we going to do if this turns out to be a disease with no cure? What if there are no further options?"

"Andrés, medicine is always about options," he answered. "We'll figure out what they are."

Third clue: ED plus immune deficiency

Within a day, Mary Kaye Richter of the National Foundation for Ectodermal Dysplasia emailed back:

> "Your son's infection history is not typical of most people affected by ectodermal dysplasia. I'm assuming Andy's got hypohydrotic ectodermal dysplasia (HED), the most common form (sparse hair, few teeth, inability to perspire) and if so, he should be evaluated for a type of HED that includes immunosuppression. I can give you the name of the physician doing genetic work in that area..."

I immediately called her number, listed at the bottom of her email. Mary

Kaye was warm and professional. She told me about a researcher, Dr. Jonathan Zonana at Oregon Health Sciences University, who was doing some tests with kids who had hypohydrotic ectodermal dysplasia as well as histories of multiple infections. He was looking for specific genetic mutations to perhaps identify another form of ED syndrome. She gave me his contact information. Finally, she mentioned that her own ED son was now 22 and enjoying a good life. "I trust that can be true for Andy as well," she said.

God bless you, I thought. Then I paged Jordan Orange. Together we contacted Dr. Zonana on my computer, as Paulina watched. Dr. Zonana emailed us back almost immediately and agreed to add Andy to his study. The research agreement he attached absolved him of any obligation to share results with us, and there was no guarantee the results would be correct. *"It's a very experimental study,"* he wrote.

Even with no guarantees, this was the most significant development since Andy's first infection. I had to pace the hallway for a few minutes, I was so agitated. Back in the room, Dr. Orange took more blood samples from Andy and Paulina to send to Dr. Zonana's lab.

"Why don't you need Andrés' blood sample too?" Paulina asked him.

"There are some genetic conditions that are known as X-linked, meaning the parent with the double X chromosomes, the female, is the carrier," Dr. Orange explained. "Boys have one X chromosome and one Y chromosome. Girls have two X chromosomes. Let's suppose Paulina has chromosomes Xa and Xb and you, Andrés, have chromosomes Xc and Yd. Andy got one chromosome from Paulina and one from Andrés. Let's suppose that Paulina's chromosome Xa has a mutation. If Andy has that Xa chromosome then he gets the mutation. He doesn't have another X to cover him. Girls have another X that can cover the mutation. They are only carriers, they are not affected."

"Then I could be a carrier for what is affecting Andy, including the ED," Paulina said slowly.

"Yes," he answered.

She looked at me, stricken, and I knew what she was thinking. I put my arm around her. *"No es tu culpa,"* I murmured. "It's not your fault."

The next day Dr. Orange came in with an article he found in the *American Journal of Human Genetics*, published just a few weeks earlier. The title read: "A Novel X-linked Disorder of Immune Deficiency and Hypohydrotic Ectodermal Dysplasia Due to Mutations in IKK-Gamma (NEMO)" The author was Jonathan Zonana, MD, the researcher we'd just talked to.

"I'm on my way to a bunch of meetings, but see what you can make of this," he said. "I'll help you with it later if it's heavy going."

I struggled with its technical language, but I could understand that Zonana had studied four boys with both ED and immunodeficiency. I learned that NEMO stands for Nuclear Factor Kappa B Essential Modulator, a major on/off switch in the immune system. I also learned that of the four cases in the article, all the participants had died of multiple and chronic infections. My heart raced. *NEMO sounds like a death sentence. This can't be what Andy has; we just need to fix his stomach.*

I left our room and went to the Harvard Medical Coop bookstore across the street. There I found several textbooks on immune deficiencies.

"Although there are no cures for immune deficiency disorders, there are several treatments in addition to the drastic option of total isolation from exposure to any microbial agent," I read. Total isolation, sealed in a germ-free environment, unable to touch another living thing. John Travolta's character in *The Boy in the Plastic Bubble* movie had made a big impression on me as a kid. The text continued,

"The treatment options include:

• Replacement of a missing protein: Immunoglobulin is the classic course of treatment.

• Replacement of a missing cell or cell line: Replacing immune stem cells via bone marrow transplantation from a genetically matching donor has a high success rate.

• Replacement of a missing or defective gene."

No description of how to replace a missing gene.

I didn't share what I'd read with Paulina.

In the meantime, Dr. Orange suggested contacting some immune deficiency organizations for more information and support. The Jeffrey Modell Foundation in New York was a great example. Vicki and Fred Modell established the charity after losing their son to a primary immune deficiency. They dedicated their lives to helping other families affected by the disease. Looking at their website, I was inspired. Why not create my own website with Andy's medical information—maybe there'd be someone else out there like the Modells who could help us? And what better way to keep our family and friends informed?

Andy's website, registered www.andy.org.mx, went live on November 20,

2000. Immediately, we started receiving messages on the guestbook.

> *Hi Andy, What a beautiful baby you are. God bless you and your family.* Carol Gonzalez

> *Hi Paulina, Andrés and Andrécito, I am happy that this new technology will work for you. We will stay more in touch and want you to know I'll keep asking about you. I love you very much. Aunt Maguis*

> *Andrés and Paulina, You and your child are always in our prayers. He seems very sweet and alert. May God look after you. Your cousins, Frank and Mona Lucido*

> *Andrécito and his parents have been a great lesson for me. You are part of me and I admire the strength and love you have shown in tackling everything. God is great. I love you very much. Aunt Ana José*

> *To Andy, my champion:*
>
> *Thanks for not giving in and now knowing your diagnosis it will be easier to move forward. Remember that you will always have my love and support. Love, Fer*

They raised our spirits and helped us feel less alone.

Magic bullet?

As soon as Andy finished another course of antivirals, we returned to Mexico to wait for the results from the ectodermal dysplasia gene test and Dr. Zonana's immune deficiency tests. Our families joyfully embraced us. Our beautiful apartment was waiting. But the real progress on Andy's condition would be happening elsewhere.

A few weeks later, I arranged a conference call so Dr. Orange could give Kretschmer and me an update. Orange's lab had managed to grow Andy's blood cells for testing. One test showed that his natural killer cells, usually unresponsive, had reacted to a dose of Interleukin-2.

"IL-2 is a naturally-occurring molecule in the immune system," Dr. Orange told us. "It's instrumental in the body's response to microbial infection, and in helping the immune system distinguish between foreign bodies and self. It's possible that supplementing Andy's immune system with IL-2 could help make up for his immune deficiency."

"Great! Let's put Andy on IL-2," I said.

"Well, it's an interesting finding, but not that simple," responded Dr. Orange. "IL-2 has been used therapeutically in adults, but it's never tested in children. Could be risky."

"However, this could be the ace up our sleeve if Andy gets into trouble again," commented Kretschmer.

Dr. Orange also told us his tests confirmed that Andy's immune system was most vulnerable to the herpes virus family, which was everywhere. The viruses included varicella, like chicken pox, and our nemesis, *cytomegalovirus*.

In addition, his lab would be investigating Andy's connection to NEMO— the fatal disease I didn't want to think about. Everything was waiting on the NEMO gene tests from Dr. Zonana, which were weeks away from being final.

Still, it was progress, and identifying IL-2 as a possible therapy was the most positive news in a while. Paulina got so excited, then had to swallow her disappointment when I told her it wasn't clear that it was safe. More tears. This time, I could comfort her—at last, it seemed doors were opening, options were appearing and we could set our sights on a diagnostic breakthrough.

It was now the end of November. When Andy developed severe diarrhea again, and blood in his diaper, I was in denial. "He's been doing better, it could be just a temporary flare up." But Paulina was insistent, and, as usual, she was right. Once again we headed for Hospital ABC. Another *cytomegalovirus* infection. We spent Christmas in the hospital, and didn't come home again until December 30.

Chapter Nine
Diagnosis Bingo

A phone call on January 25, 2001 changed everything.

"Hello, Andrés, Jordan Orange here. I have some news. You know that finding the genetic roots of any disease really increases the options for finding treatments and cures, right?" His normally calm voice had a higher pitch—he was excited.

"Yes, I understand." What was he getting at?

"Dr. Zonana called me. He finally found Andy *has* the NEMO mutation—it's on the fourth exon of Andy's NEMO gene. This could be the answer we've been looking for, a key reason that Andy can't fight infection. We've got some major pieces of the puzzle now."

"Oh my God! Are you sure? What does it mean?" I was overwhelmed with hope and confusion "What do we do now? How can this help Andy get better?"

"First, I want you to return to Boston while I rerun the test here to confirm the findings," said Orange. "Then we need to consider what are the options for boosting Andy's immune system, especially knowing what we do about his susceptibility to varicella viruses. We need to find the best way to maintain him while we continue looking for the best treatment."

I was elated and Paulina wanted to pack our bags on the spot. But before we could return to Boston, Andy hit another crisis.

VZIG relay

On February 11, we took Andy across town to visit my sister Veronica and her family. She now had three kids, and the youngest, Dani, was just 6 months old. Andy loved to be around his cousins, watching their antics from his stroller.

The next day Vero called, her voice anxious. Dani had just been diagnosed with chicken pox, which meant Andy had been exposed to the dreaded varicella virus.

I immediately called Dr. Orange. His advice was swift. "Andy needs VZIG—varicella-zoster immune globulin—right away. VZIG can minimize symptoms if given soon enough. He'll have to get an infusion before the end of tomorrow."

I leapt into action, while Paulina kept a sharp eye on Andy for any signs of fever. I called every local pharmacy, then Dr. Vazquez at ABC. No one had VZIG. Finally, I called Kretschmer.

"You're not going to find that drug here," he said. "Best bet is the US."

So we turned to our old friend, the pharmacist-smuggler from Monterrey. He agreed to drive into Texas for the medication, a five-hour round trip. Then we'd need a courier from Monterrey to Mexico City. I called my Monterrey friend René, who offered to pick up the delivery from the pharmacist and take it to the airport, if we could find someone for the Mexico City leg of the relay.

Paulina had a long list of friends in Monterrey, where she'd gone to college. She sent out an email, *"Urgencia médica"*, to see if anyone was flying to our city that night. Miraculously, she found Adriana, who was taking the 7:00 p.m. Aeromexico flight.

The pharmacist called from McAllen, Texas, "I found the VZIG and I should be back in Monterrey by 5 p.m."

Paulina and I worked both our cell phones to keep track of that tiny box. René picked it up at the pharmacy at 6:30, arrived at the airport at 6:55 and sprinted for the gate, keeping me connected by phone. The plane had already boarded, the jetway was shut. René, panting, handed his cell phone to the startled woman at the ticket counter so I could explain to her why the little package of VZIG needed to get to Adriana on the plane.

"Please, this is to save a baby's life," I begged.

The woman radioed the flight captain and examined the package. "I hope I don't get in trouble for this," she said, as the crew reconnected the jetway and Adriana retrieved the box.

"*¡Señorita, usted se va a ir al cielo!* Miss, you're going to heaven!" I answered.

"We managed to delay an Aeromexico flight!" I boasted to Paulina. I was still feeling the adrenaline high as I drove to the airport to meet Adriana.

Andy got the VZIG infusion at Hospital ABC the next day. But I felt helpless when, within hours, he started coughing and his fever spiked. He had pneumonia, an infection probably caused by the varicella. It was torture to watch his labored breathing. Paulina kept complaining it made her own chest ache.

I called Dr. Orange again. "Andy's in serious trouble. What about starting him on IL-2?" I asked.

"I'm sorry, Andrés, we can't do that without getting permission to establish a pediatric protocol, with appropriate follow up," he answered. "And it will have to be done here in Boston. I'll get started setting it up—it'll take about a week. In the meantime, I still think Andy's condition would be worse without the VZIG. Try giving him a second dose, and hang in there. I'll see you here at Children's as soon as Andy can travel."

After seven nerve-wracking days, Andy's breathing eased. He started to smile again. I lost no time making travel arrangements for Boston.

A miracle drug?

On March 10, 2001, we met Dr. Orange at Children's Hospital's clinical research department to sign the legal consents to the protocol. Andy would receive a five-day infusion of IL-2, in a "compassionate use" clinical trial. Which meant it was a big experiment. We were in uncharted waters—no one really knew how much of the drug to give a child. Frequent blood tests were necessary to monitor side effects, which included, ironically, a decrease in white blood cell count. But we signed eagerly.

There was an unexpected bonus—the hospital's grant funding for this clinical study covered our stay. We settled into a room on the 7th floor, where our nurse, Erin, immediately pursed her mouth and sucked in her cheeks, making a "fish face." Andy laughed for the first time in weeks.

The room's previous tenants had painted the glass window on the hallway with lollipops and gumdrops and big lettering:

CANDY LAND

I took a wet paper towel and rubbed off the first letter.

ANDY LAND

Trouble dogged us. We couldn't begin the infusion because a CT scan showed Andy's lungs were still recovering from the pneumonia. Worse, he'd developed a deep abscess near his rectum that was nearly impossible to keep clean, dry and medicated, especially when another bout of *C. difficile* infection brought constant diarrhea. He had surgery to help it drain, and through trial and error, our nurses helped us find the best way to treat his abscess—painting the lesion with liquid antacid and drying it with a small electric fan.

"If I ever hear any other mother complain about diaper rash, I'm going to give her a swift kick," Paulina muttered.

For the next 10 days we were sleepless robots driven by a single program: keeping Andy's pain at bay. He screamed and kicked at every diaper change, every 20 minutes. We were desperate for anything to divert his attention. The window in our room looked out at the rooftop heliport on Brigham and Women's Hospital next door and medi-flight landings became Andy's primary distraction. As soon as he heard the chopper, even in mid-howl, he'd lift his arms to be carried to the window. And he developed a special friendship with a clinical assistant named Elaina, a gentle African American woman who seemed to intuit his moods and needs. He would calm down listening to her soft voice, telling him what a brave, special boy he was.

Dr. Nurko was managing all of Andy's gastrointestinal treatment; Dr. Orange came by twice a day; and daily teams of surgical residents made the room feel like a fishbowl. Once we received a visit from Dr. Raif Geha, the chief of Immunology and Kretschmer's old friend. "I have high hopes for this IL-2 treatment," he told us. *If we ever get to try it,* I thought.

Finally, Andy's condition improved enough to start the infusion, two weeks late. Paulina and I were so exhausted it was an extra effort to feel anything, even relief.

The infusion lasted five days. By then, Andy's stomach seemed stable so we flew home to wait for the next steps.

Back in Mexico, it was hard to respond as our families asked about our stay and the treatment. We just couldn't share how nightmarish it had been. Over the next few weeks, we waited for the IL-2 to take effect, praying to see any sign it was helping him fight infection. The anal fissure still refused to heal. And in the second week of April, another *C. difficile* infection struck—Andy's vomiting and diarrhea were relentless, and he began to look emaciated again. He needed Vancomycin, and, of course, there was none in Mexico.

Enough. I bought one-way tickets to Boston. On April 24, my parents took us to the airport, hugged us at the gate, their faces somber. "So, when are you coming back?" my mother asked.

"I think we're going to be staying until he's cured," Paulina answered, busying herself with our luggage, her voice unsteady.

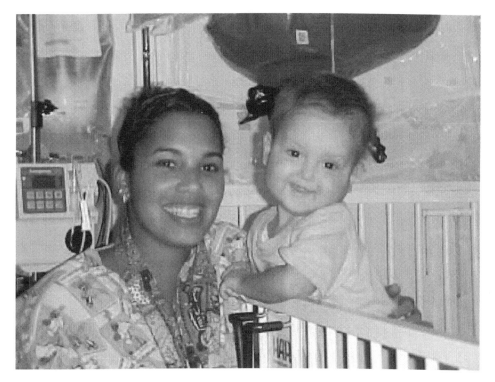

Andy with nurse Ruth at Children's Hospital Boston.

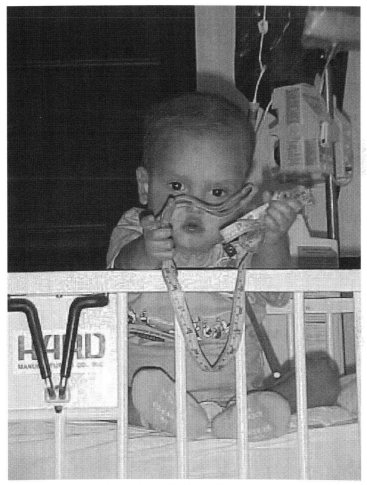

Andy playing with his "aii" (measuring tape.)

Chapter Ten
Boston for Good

On arrival we went straight to Children's Emergency Department and were admitted to the 7 East floor again. Our friends—nurse Erin and clinical assistant Elaina—greeted us with open arms, and Andy held out his own arms with a big smile. Dr. Nurko showed up and took charge, ordering more X-rays and blood tests. Jordan Orange soon followed, and we all sat together on the sofa bed while Elaina played peekaboo with Andy. We asked Jordan why it was taking so long for his lab to confirm the NEMO diagnosis, and why the IL-2 hadn't worked. When would we break this stalemate and get the answers we needed?

"It may take repeated doses for IL-2 to take effect," he said. "This is still an experiment. As soon as his infection is under control, we can try it again." He put his hand on my shoulder. "I know this all feels like a waiting game, and it's hard to just keep taking one day at a time. But the big picture is coming into focus—soon."

A day in the life

On April 26, my parents called to wish me a happy 30th birthday. It was my mother's birthday, too, and I'd forgotten, for the first time ever.

Paulina's 28th birthday a few weeks later was even less celebratory. Here are my notes:

Date: Sunday, May 6, 2001

Where: Children's Hospital Boston 7th Floor East

2:00 a.m.: The nurse enters the room to give Andy a dose of Vancomycin for the C. difficile via his stomach tube. He sleeps through it.

6:00 a.m.: The nurse comes in to take a blood sample. We ask her to come back when Andy's awake.

"Happy Birthday," I tell Paulina, and give her a kiss.

6:44 a.m.: The feeding pump alarm goes off — the formula's finished. We decide to turn off the pump and halt his continuous night feeding 15 minutes early rather than have a nurse come in right now and refill it. I hold Paulina tight and whisper, "You are 28 years old today, the most beautiful woman in the world." She giggles and pokes me in the ribs.

7:30 a.m.: The nurse enters the room to tell us she has to take blood samples to measure electrolytes and do an allergy test. Andy's still asleep, so we ask the nurse to do it later. I'm still holding Paulina and don't want to let her go.

8:45 a.m.: Andy wakes, calls to us. I get up and change his diaper and he winces and whimpers while I clean the open lesion on his bottom.

9:00 a.m.: The nurse enters the room to check Andy's vital signs. She takes his temperature, blood pressure and blood oxygen levels.

9:15 a.m.: The nurse tries to take blood from Andy's central line for the blood test. Neither of the double catheter lines yields blood.

9:30 a.m.: The nurse tries to take blood via a needle in his arm, as Andy wails. She obtains only 3 ml; 5 are required. The remaining blood tests are left for tomorrow.

10:00 a.m.: Andy's fussing, and keeps pulling at his right shoulder where his catheter is placed. We request a bandage change. When the nurse takes the gauze off, the catheter site is swollen and oozing. Another infection, but is it a new one or a return of the previous one? The nurse pages the physician-on-call.

10:30 a.m.: It's time for Andy's tube feeding, but after a couple of minutes he vomits.

11:00 a.m.: The doctor examines the catheter site and decides to consult the surgeon-on-call.

11:15 a.m.: A team of gastroenterologists enters the room to evaluate the catheter. They also decide to consult the surgeon.

11:30 a.m.: The surgeon examines Andy's shoulder and decides to pull the catheter. He takes the catheter tip to culture the latest infection.

11:45 a.m.: Andy falls asleep for a little while, so I run down to get breakfast from the café in the hospital lobby.

11:50 a.m.: Andy vomits. We change the crib sheets.

12:00 p.m.: The nurse wants to prepare Andy for an IV. It's been so difficult to find a vein, she asks us to take him to the treatment room. Andy vomits while I'm carrying him.

12:10 p.m.: Paulina takes a shower while I'm with Andy in the treatment room.

12:15 p.m.: The nurse tries an IV on Andy's toe, unsuccessfully. Paulina tidies up the sofa-bed, and then joins us in the treatment room. I leave to take a shower.

12:20 p.m.: The nurse tries an IV in Andy's right arm, then his left arm, with no luck. Andy's wailing. Paulina's almost crying too, asks the nurse to let Andy rest, try again later. Andy vomits on Paulina's shirt.

12:30 p.m.: Andy sleeps a bit. Paulina changes into a fresh shirt and she and I eat our now-stale breakfast in the room. A gastroenterologist enters, tells us that she asked an anesthesiologist to try the IV again. We ask her to let us know when we should head to the treatment room.

12:45 p.m.: A priest from the hospital's chaplaincy program knocks, offering prayer and communion. We accept.

1:00 p.m.: Andy needs to eat, and we try to feed him through his stomach tube, but he vomits. The nurse calls the physician-on-call and they decide to change the feeding formula to Pedialyte—Andy's dehydrated and losing electrolytes. We ask the doctor about Andy's medicines and discover that the anti-diarrhea medication is probably causing the nausea and vomiting. The doctor orders the Imodium discontinued. Andy vomits again.

1:30 p.m.: The anesthesiologist arrives and asks us to take Andy to the treatment room. Paulina holds Andy and takes a seat. The doctor tries to find a vein in Andy's foot. No luck. He makes an unsuccessful attempt at the right arm, then with the left. Andy's screaming and Paulina's frustration is mounting. "I could do a better job!" she hisses to me. Finally the anesthesiologist manages to prick a vein enough to get a blood sample.

2:00 p.m.: We return to the room. Andy's still dehydrated—he's crying without tears. He needs fluids, so we suggest trying an IV on his scalp. The nurse prepares the treatment room again.

2:30 p.m.: This time, I take Andy to the treatment room, while Paulina fields phone calls from family in Mexico. "Oh, thank you, yes, everything's fine here, I'm having a nice birthday." She cuts the phone calls short, goes to the communal laundry room to wash our dirty clothes. The anesthesiologist asks me for my shaving razor. He shaves a patch of Andy's head near the ear and inserts the IV into a blood vessel. Then he realizes the IV's in an artery, not a vein. He removes the IV. Andy cries the whole time.

3:00 p.m.: We're still in the treatment room. The physician-on-call arrives with a neo-natologist and a lamp. I recognize the neonatologist—it's Dr. Paul Lerou, the young resident who was doing rounds when we first learned about Andy's ectodermal dysplasia. He uses the lamp to locate a vein in Andy's arm, and successfully inserts the IV. Andy stops crying.

3:30 p.m.: We return to our room. The nurse begins the IV saline infusion and takes Andy's temperature, blood pressure and blood oxygen. Paulina goes to the laundry room to pick up our clothes.

4:00 p.m.: The nurse comes in and starts the IV pump for his antibiotic infusion. It's also time for Andy's Pedialyte through his stomach tube. He vomits.

4:30 p.m.: Andy loses his IV—it falls out of his arm when he flails during a diaper change. The nurse calls the physician-on-call, who calls the neonatologist again.

5:00 p.m.: We take Andy back to the treatment room, Dr. Lerou again is successful with the IV.

5:30 p.m.: Back in our room, the nurse gives Andy a saline infusion.

6:00 p.m.: Andy naps, and we fall asleep, too.

6:15 p.m.: I apparently sleepwalk, placing a (harmless) clip on Andy's stomach tube.

6:30 p.m.: The beeper on the pump signals the end of the stomach tube feeding. We wake; Paulina discovers, inexplicably, there's a clip on Andy's stomach tube.

6:35 p.m.: The physician-on-call is concerned about the vomiting and dehydration, requests an x-ray of Andy's stomach.

6:45 p.m.: Andy vomits. While we change his bed sheets, the hospital's fire alarm goes off and the door to the room shuts automatically. The loudspeaker tells everyone there's a fire on the second floor.

6:50 p.m.: We can hear the firefighter's sirens outside the building. Then the loud-speaker announces a false alarm. The portable x-ray machine arrives to get an image of Andy's stomach. As usual, he gives a big smile for the "camera."

7:00 p.m.: The nurses change shifts. I go to the lobby café to buy lunch. Or is it dinner?

7:30 p.m.: We have turkey sandwiches and tomato soup for dinner. I lift a can of soda to Paulina, "Happy Birthday." Andy vomits again.

8:00 p.m.: Andy wails as he receives his daily intramuscular shots—simultaneously in each thigh. The two nurses hate administering it, but they love comforting Andy afterwards.

8:30 p.m.: The on-call doctors review Andy's chart and want to rule out whether he has an intestinal occlusion. We agree to let them open the stomach tube valve and empty his stomach. No blockage. Andy feels better immediately.

8:35 p.m.: Paulina takes him for a walk in his stroller along the 7th floor corridor. Andy says "hi" to everyone they pass.

8:45 p.m.: Back in the room, the nurse takes Andy's temperature, blood pressure and blood oxygen. Andy gets an intravenous nutrition feeding—no more stomach feedings for a while.

9:00 p.m.: Lying in his crib, Andy plays with his "aiii"—his tape measure⌐ ⌐—until he's drowsy. We're already in our sweatpants and t-shirts. We can't wait for the next few hours of sleep.

Andy turns 2

On the morning of May 15, Andy's second birthday, I woke and calculated: 731 days since the beginning of our ordeal.

Jordan Orange, his wife, Katie, and their baby daughter Audrey surprised us with a cake, presents and balloons, so we turned the 7th floor playroom into a party space. I knew the Oranges' kindness was as much for Paulina and me as for Andy, and I couldn't thank them enough. Our nursing friends, the Child Life specialists and even the hospital's resident clowns all dropped by. Andy wasn't so sure about the clowns and hid his face in my shoulder. More than anything, he was delighted to play with Audrey on a mat on the floor. He could sit up by himself now, so he was right at Audrey's level in terms of physical development, even though he was more than a year older. He had some color in his cheeks and enough baby roundness from the intravenous feedings to look like a regular two-year-old, but in miniature. Chronic illness had robbed his body of any extra energy to grow.

It pained me that he had so little interaction with other kids—with anyone other than caregivers, really. For all the alternating stress and tedium we felt, Andy's experience was so much worse. He just was starting to speak—"Mama," "Papa" and "Aimee," his favorite nurse. Months ago we'd taught him enough sign language to be able to tell us when he was tired, hungry or wanting to be held. He touched his left hand to his forehead if he wanted to go for a stroll in the corridor. He held his hands in a circle if he wanted to play ball. He was so pleased with himself when he could make his few demands and get a response.

Nowhere to go

By the time we were ready to be discharged, Andy was starting the Interleukin-2 again. Paulina and I had to learn to give him the IL-2 shots three times a week ourselves. We practiced on each other using syringes of water—Paulina kept giggling, knowing how needles used to make me faint. Andy would need weekly follow up with Dr. Nurko and Dr. Orange. We couldn't return to Mexico.

"We're so close to finding answers, I don't even want to think about going back," Paulina said, even though I knew she was terribly homesick. I found us an apartment sub-lease in nearby Watertown for the summer, and arranged to have our jeep delivered from Mexico City—cheaper than a rental car. I got a little charge driving around Boston in the only car with Mexico City plates.

We left the hospital on May 23, a beautiful spring morning, and Boston was in full bloom as we took a walk with Andy in his stroller along the Charles River. He kept holding his hands out to the pink clouds of flowering crabapples, his eyes squinting in the sun, his face full of wonder. After months inside a hospital room, he was thrilled to see leaves and trees again. *"Hojas. Arboles,"* we told him, our hearts full. At that moment, his joy was all we needed.

I was delighted when Paulina's cousin Ivonne agreed to come to stay with us for the summer to help out. Suddenly we had the unbelievable luxury of a few hours to ourselves on a regular basis, to rest and recharge together. Still, Paulina bore the brunt of Andy's care, maintaining his medication and feeding schedule. Andy had been bedridden for so long he qualified for early intervention services—physical, occupational and speech therapy, so he had plenty of appointments, which he considered "playing." He loved learning. We'd been so focused on teaching him how to cooperate with injections and blood draws we'd forgotten to show him colors and shapes, letters and numbers.

Meanwhile, I tried to figure out ways to raise money. The Neocate formula cost about $40 per day, and it wasn't covered by our insurance. The IL-2 also was ferociously expensive. First, I focused on getting our Mexico City apartment rented. Paulina shed a few tears over the home we'd chosen and decorated with so much love and anticipation. My mother, Marilu, my sister, Veronica, and Paulina's aunt, Ana José, all pitched in to pack and store all of our belongings, sparing us the cost and anxiety of another trip. Then I turned to selling customized baseball caps, embroidered with www.andy.org. mx, through our website. Given another opportunity to help us, our family-and-friends network once again stepped up to the plate.

Is it terminal?

Andy was in and out of the hospital through June and July with persistent ulcerative colitis—painful lesions in his gut that kept him from absorbing adequate nutrition. The new medication to treat the inflammation, Imuran, helped calm his digestive system and hopefully would allow him to get stronger. But Imuran was also an immune-suppressant. I was worried. The IL-2 didn't seem to help the chronic intestinal condition, and if his immune system was further compromised what would prevent a new wave of opportunistic infection?

One morning in July, when Jordan Orange came in for his daily visit, I invited him to walk down the hall with me.

"Jordan, how many NEMO cases are out there?"

"Only about 15—and they're all different from Andy's. He's the only case we know of where the mutation's on the NEMO gene's fourth exon. We know he's vulnerable to herpes/varicella viruses, and in my lab we're trying to understand what else is affected."

"But right now, as things stand—is Andy's condition considered incurable? Is it…terminal?"

We'd reached a small, empty lounge with a faded couch and a plastic chair. Jordan paused and looked directly at me. "Yes."

It shouldn't have been a surprise—still, I felt as though I'd been kicked in the gut. I sat on the couch, he took the chair. "What do we do now?"

He leaned forward. "Andrés, believe me, there are still options. Let me pull my thoughts together and meet with you and Paulina tonight so we can talk about it."

Andy's 2nd birthday party with grandfather Alfredo, grandmother Lupita holding Audrey Orange, Andrés and Andy at Children's Hospital Boston.

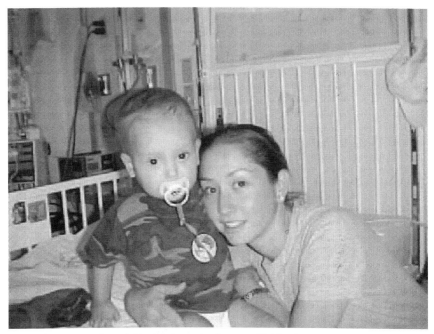

Andy with Paulina's cousin, Ivonne, Children's Hospital Boston

PART THREE

THE RACE FOR A DONOR

A MARATHON, NOT A SPRINT

Chapter Eleven
The 12.5 percent solution

That evening, Jordan Orange entered our room holding a pad and pen, and the three of us perched on the sofa bed. Andy was sleeping. Without mentioning the word "terminal," I'd told Paulina Dr. Orange was going to talk to us about options. I was both tense and exhausted, and as Paulina leaned against me I tried to slow my breathing to match hers.

"Let's review," he began. "As you know, when Dr. Zonana from the University of Oregon examined Andy's cells, he found mutations on the fourth part of the NEMO gene, something he'd never seen before." He opened the pad and began sketching boxes and circles and arrows.

"Each cell nucleus holds DNA, which carries genes, which in turn make proteins. The gene proteins are comprised of amino acids. Think of a protein as an opera recording that includes, say, 420 songs. Let's suppose that each song from the opera represents one amino acid. Turns out that Andy's opera is missing one song, he's missing song number 153."

He had our full attention.

"Our objective has been to understand what type of opera is playing and the effect the missing song has on the whole production. We needed to know the function of that song or amino acid number 153 and how it affects Andy's immune system."

Jordan continued, "First we verified that the NEMO mutation was real. Sometimes we find pseudo genes that give false results. The next step was to see which cell activities were affected by amino acid 153. In Andy's case, it was the natural killer cell response, the one that attacks invading organisms first."

"Yes, that goes back to the first clue last October," murmured Paulina. "He and I have bad NK cells."

"So, we confirmed the theory that the mutation on the NEMO gene was causing an immune deficiency," said Jordan. "We discovered that his condition affects his NK cells, but could have bigger implications as well."

"Then we found that IL-2 could be an option to boost his immune response. It worked very well on NK cells in the lab but real life can be another story and that's why you're still in the hospital. It's clear now that IL-2 isn't enough to help his immune system, which is too defective. There's no known drug that can save Andy."

He paused and looked directly at us. "But there is a treatment that might work."

Paulina sat up straight. I forgot I was tired.

He continued. "Today I spoke to Dr. Geha, our Immunology chief, and he recommends a stem cell transplant for Andy. We'd use chemotherapy to destroy his bone marrow, where his faulty blood cells are made, and replace it with new blood stem cells from another person—a donor. The transplanted cells would attach and build a new, healthy immune system. It's a risky procedure, but it's really Andy's only chance. There's no risk or harm to a stem cell donor, of course, but they have to be a genetic match for it to work at all."

"How do you measure a genetic match?" Paulina asked. "Where would we find someone with matching genes?"

"We run a blood test called human leukocyte antigen, or HLA, that analyzes a series of molecules, looking for very specific compatibilities. For this kind of treatment, there needs to be a 100 percent match—anything less won't work. The most compatible donor is likely to be a brother or sister."

"You mean *my* brother or sister?" I was confused. "Couldn't I be a donor?"

"No, no, since you and Paulina each contributed half of Andy's genes, you're each only 50 percent compatible. Other family members are likely to be even less so. The best chance for a full genetic match would be *Andy's* sibling."

"But Andy doesn't have a…oh." I was starting to get the picture. Paulina was already ahead of me.

"So we need to make another baby," she said. "A baby who could give some healthy blood cells." Her face, flushed and bright-eyed, told me she was getting interested. When we were courting, Paulina and I had talked about wanting at least three children. Living with Andy's illness had dashed those dreams. We had a hard time thinking about taking care of second child, let alone the possibility of getting another baby with a fatal disease.

"Yes, that's right," Jordan answered. "At the baby's birth, we'd store the umbilical cord blood, which contains blood stem cells. You've heard of stem cells, right? They're cells with two unique qualities–they can make endless copies of themselves and they can mature into a variety of specialized cells. So the cord blood is rich in hematopoietic stem cells, the same kind of blood-producing cells that are in bone marrow. Hematopoietic cells can turn into all the types of blood cells the immune system needs. They'd be capable of generating that entire range of blood cells if they were transfused into Andy, once his old, defective immune system was destroyed by chemotherapy. We call it a transplant because the stem cells would actually attach in the bone marrow and begin to produce a whole new immune system. Like having a new heart, or a new liver. Andy would be permanently cured."

My heart leapt. I was starting to get excited, too.

"Now, here's the key issue," he continued. "You could get pregnant and wait to see if the baby is compatible. There's a 50 percent chance it would be a boy, 50 percent it would be a girl. But we're dealing with more than just the gender issue. We're also dealing with the HLA compatibility issue, so there's only a 25 percent chance this boy or girl would have the same combination of genes from you and Paulina that Andy has."

More drawing little stick figures on the pad.

"Now, there's also a 25 percent probability that this baby boy or girl would have the NEMO mutation. Remember, it's an X-linked disease, where boys express the disease and girls merely carry it. So if the baby boy has the mutation, he'd have the disease, like Andy. If the baby girl has the mutation, she would just be a carrier like Paulina and wouldn't have health problems. She could still be a successful donor."

"So the best option would be a sister," I said, my mind churning. "And if your numbers are correct, it sounds like we'd have a one in two chance of having a girl, a one in four chance of having an *HLA compatible* girl, and a one in eight chance of having an *HLA compatible girl without the NEMO mutation.*" And the last combination, being the NEMO carrier, isn't necessarily a deal-breaker."

"So we need to have this baby girl as soon as possible?" Paulina asked.

"We couldn't attempt a transplant unless Andy is strong enough—and infection free," said Jordan. "We'd need his stomach issues and his weight to be stable. Beyond that, most experts agree it's safer to do the procedure before age five."

"We have less than three years to produce a girl with the right stuff." I turned to Paulina. "And the chances are only one in eight."

"We'll need help," said Paulina. "Fertility treatments. How soon can we get started?"

Chapter Twelve
Baby-making

We'd heard about "test-tube babies," of course—a friend of Paulina's had undergone *in vitro* fertilization and been rewarded with triplets. But we'd been spared the details. Once we started looking, the IVF baby-making information sounded daunting. Paulina would be carefully monitored to determine her menstrual cycle's exact timing. Then she'd get a series of hormone shots to develop as many eggs as possible—20 in one cycle was not unusual. When ready, the eggs would be harvested through a needle in Paulina's abdomen, examined, and placed in culture dish. Then came my part—sperm donation into a jar. The sperm would be analyzed, and then mixed with Paulina's eggs. Normally, about 85 percent of the eggs would fertilize. Within three days, each fertilized egg would have divided into about eight cells—a very early embryo. Doctors would determine the best ones to be implanted in Paulina's womb.

The whole idea left me a bit queasy. We'd be creating a baby without sex. But not without love. And whether created by medical technology or ordinary lovemaking, no one really knows exactly what makes an embryo attach to the wall of the uterus and grow. It was luck or grace. We needed lots of both.

While we were still in the hospital with Andy, two Children's geneticists, Dr. Natasha Frank and Dr. David Harris, came to talk to us about pre-implantation genetic diagnosis, or PGD. This is the method of screening IVF embryos for genetic traits *before* they were implanted in the womb. It sounded like science fiction, but apparently the test could now be done without harming the embryo's development. In our case, we'd need two tests—one for the HLA match Jordan had told us about, and another to test for NEMO. But the NEMO diagnosis was so new, a test didn't exist—it would have to be created. Dr. Frank showed us a list of the 11 pre-implantation genetic diagnosis centers in the US, and she offered to email them all in the hopes of finding one who'd take on our case and create the test. It would be months before we received an answer.

The summer proceeded in slow motion. We were in and out of the hospital every few weeks with Andy's colitis flare-ups and the painful rectal abscess he'd had since February. When our summer sublet was up, I found a two-bed-room apartment in Waltham, about 40 minutes from the hospital. By August, Cousin Ivonne returned home, and we were on our own taking care of Andy.

Despite our exhaustion, Paulina was impatient to get her pregnancy start-ed. "This is the solution—I know it, I prayed for it. Andrés, it's going to give us the two things we've wanted most: Andy cured and living like a normal little boy, and another baby to love. After we thought we couldn't have any more kids." Her eyes filled.

"Yes, I know, but it's going to be a long road to put all the pieces together. And if we do reach that point, it's still going to be a drastic procedure, danger-ous for Andy. I wish...I just wish there was some other way..."

Her tears spilled. "This is all *my* fault. My body, my genetic mutation, did this to our son."

I drew her close. "It's *not* your fault! It's no one's fault. I have genetic flaws, everyone does, and some are more harmful than others. It's not your fault, Paulina."

To help pass the long, tedious hours in the hospital, I read everything I could find about IVF, PGD, stem cell transplants and gene therapy. When the time came, I wanted to be able to explain it to our families and have it make as much sense to them as it did to me.

I kept my spirits up through our website. I'd made a poster for our hospi-tal window, visible to passersby on the sidewalk of Longwood Avenue:

PLEASE HELP.

VISIT www.andy.org.mx.

I asked everyone who visited the site to join a bone marrow registry. I needed to feel I was doing *something* to put out the word about our dilemma, even if all we got back were encouraging messages from strangers.

> *Hi Andy! Our daughter, Hana, met you at Children's Hospital Boston in the 8 East Playroom. You made her smile with your big smile. You were showing off your new blue sneakers and seemed very proud. It was very nice to meet you and we wish you best wishes for a cure and a long happy life. Take care!! Amy, Peter and Hana*

And I posted news to friends and family almost every day.

August 20, 2001

Andy has been doing better since last Thursday, when we left the hospital. For now, each day he looks healthier—I still hope that he'll get strong enough not to need so many hospitalizations. We're still giving him IL-2 shots on Mondays, Wednesdays and Fridays—Paulina's better at this than I am—no surprise. Andy now gets gamma globulin every three weeks instead of every four.

Last week, they took seven vials of blood from us in order to start mapping out our genetics. We'll be asking you all to get your blood tested too—in case there's a match that's close enough.

Some doctors tell us that the blood stem cell transplant may not be the best option. Sometimes it's not successful and children going through a transplant suffer a lot. I struggle with this. We'd love it if Andy were able to remain infection-free on fewer medications, but we may never reach that point. Paulina is incredibly strong; she impresses me every day.

Sept 1, 2001

We were discharged from the hospital last Sunday with some changes in medication (details below.) Andy still has some stomach pain, heartburn and nausea; he still doesn't sleep well at night, sometimes waking up every 20 minutes. We're trying to stay focused on finding the best combination of feeding times, antacids and formulas to help him gain weight without creating discomfort.

We try to take advantage of his days out of the hospital. Andy loves being walked around outdoors in his stroller, and feeding ducks on the Charles River always makes him happy. He's starting to use more words, he can say "quack quack" and points out "leaves" and "flowers" and "trees."

We're still hoping for the transplant. Even though we've received conflicting opinions from different doctors, we now believe it's the best way to go. The most important aspect is finding the right donor. We'll continue searching for an existing donor, but everyone agrees our best chance is to create a little sister whose umbilical cord stem cells could be used for the transplant.

The roller coaster

I couldn't see how adding IVF treatments would make our lives any more difficult. But the fall of 2001 tested us further. We were in the hospital with Andy on September 11, a terrible day of fear, confusion and grief. Like everyone, we were glued to the TV, watching the terrorist attack on the World Trade Center over and over, forgetting that Andy, sitting in his crib, could see the screen too. By the end of the day, he was shaping his hands like airplanes and waving them through the air. We angled the screen, muted the sound and made sure we monitored his TV exposure after that. Children's Hospital was on crisis alert, expecting to receive any pediatric attack victims that couldn't be cared for in New York or Washington. But no survivors arrived that day, or in the days that followed. We already loved our hospital home. And as we watched so many brave and generous reactions from the American people over the next few weeks, we were inspired to care about our adopted country even more.

In early October, Dr. Natasha Frank, the geneticist, emailed us at home with good news. One of the preimplantation genetic diagnosis centers she'd contacted had responded. Dr. Mark Hughes from the Center for Molecular Medicine and Genetics at Wayne State University was interested in our case. A few days later he called us.

"The first step is to find a good fertility clinic close to home," he said. "I recommend The Fertility Center of New England with Dr. Cardone and Dr. Lee—they're in Reading, Massachusetts, just north of Boston."

"Once you've gotten to the step where Paulina's harvested eggs are fertilized with Andrés' sperm *in vitro*, and start dividing, you will have gone through what all IVF couples do. Now comes the new part, where my lab steps into the picture."

I was listening so hard my ears tingled, and through the open bedroom door I watched Paulina on the kitchen phone extension, her eyes closed in concentration. Her breathing came through the line whenever Dr. Hughes paused.

"At the fertility clinic, a technician will use a micro-straw—that's 1/25 of the diameter of a human hair—to remove one cell from each blastomere. That's the eight-cell cluster that the fertilized egg becomes after about three days, which is really more like a pre-embryo," he continued. "It won't cause any damage to the embryo to remove a cell at this stage—it will more than make up for it. Early embryos are made up of stem cells that have extraordinary power to grow all the cells a human body needs—or even more. Just think how identical twins also grow out of a single dividing fertilized egg—it replicates enough to form *two* embryos. Anyway, each biopsied single cell will travel by courier to my lab here in Michigan. I'll take DNA from the cells and test it for HLA compatibility. And, just as important, I'll develop a special test so we can find out if it has the NEMO mutation, too. When we get the test results, we call the fertility clinic holding the embryos to let them know which ones, if any, could be implanted in Paulina to create a pregnancy."

I was struggling to process this description. "How can you do that, biopsy just one tiny cell? Is that enough to get the right information?"

"Look at it this way—I'll use an analogy. All the genetic information we need is contained in that cell's DNA. Written out, it would equal 300 volumes of the *Encyclopedia Britannica*. I'll use the equivalent of a molecular spell-checker to identify the one "paragraph" that could contain an error—the NEMO mutation. Thanks to research from Dr. Zonana, Dr. Orange and others, we know just where it's located. And we also know where to find the one or two 'pages' of genetic information making up the HLA type."

I had a few more questions. "How long will it take to create the test? And do you know what the success rate is for the whole procedure, from IVF to birth and getting umbilical cord blood for a transplant?"

"It will take me several weeks to set up my lab. As for the success rate, it's somewhere around 10 percent."

A one-in-ten chance. Through the phone extension I heard Paulina's breath catch. Dr. Hughes heard it too.

"For any couple, the hardest part of the whole IVF and PGD process is the emotional roller coaster, with so many different points for failure or success," he said gently. "It's especially hard for a couple like you, dealing with your son's condition at the same time. But it's the best chance we can offer."

"We know, and we thank you," I said. "Andy deserves every chance we can give him."

Before signing off, Dr. Hughes told us that out of the total PGD costs, including devising a brand-new test, we'd only have to pay for the courier service from Reading, Massachusetts to Detroit, Michigan. His laboratory would take care of the rest. After all, we were advancing his research. I called The Fertility Center of New England immediately, while Paulina joined me and listened. We secured the first available appointment, three weeks away. After I hung up I led Paulina to the couch where we held each other for a few minutes without speaking.

Faith and Belief

We'd both been brought up Catholic and attended parochial schools taught mostly by priests and nuns. I'd had the requisite years of Sunday school, preparing for my First Communion with *Padre* Chava at age 10. I'd enjoyed him and had no problem doing what was expected of me. But after that passage, I never made another confession—I just didn't believe in that whole premise. My family's not especially devout, attending church a few times a year for holidays, weddings, funerals and baptisms.

Our wedding ceremony, for example, held in Chiapas, cemented our families. It was the church connection that helped us gather more than 500 people (not a huge wedding by Mexican standards) on that one beautiful May day. Through the ritual of Catholicism they became part of our circle, to sustain us as a couple, and hopefully as a new family, with loyalty and love and hope.

Like most Mexicans I know, I view my religion as more about tradition than spiritual salvation. My personal religious beliefs have been shaped by my experience, not Church teachings. I do believe in God, as a higher force or power in the world. He's manifested in nature, and in special moments of love and wonder, like a baby's first cry. I can feel close to God sitting near a waterfall, not sitting in a pew. And I don't believe God is directing the events of my life. There are so many factors involved in what happens, some we can control or influence, some we can't. In the anguish of Andy's ordeal, we often asked ourselves, "Why is this happening to him, why is he suffering?" But we never felt it was personal, that God was deliberately causing our pain. We were seeking medical answers, not religious ones.

I've always been interested in science. During Andy's illness I'd been trying to keep up with relevant medical research. Even though it seems some things just can't be explained, phenomena that seem "miraculous" may be scientifically analyzed one day. We had a few futile experiences with psychics and faith healers brought in by various family members in Mexico, and we went along with the process to please them, but I had no patience with ignorance and superstition.

Even so, prayer is an important ritual, part of our culture. In Mexico our friends and relatives filled our hospital room with crucifixes, medals and icons of saints to pray to—and we did, both alone and with anyone who visited. Paulina repeated novenas all the time. She had a book of them her mother had given her, and she found it soothing. I prayed whenever Andy had a procedure, saying Hail Marys or Our Fathers rapidly over and over, a mental exercise that steadied my mind. Since we'd come to Boston, Children's Catholic chaplaincy staff, Father Bob and Sister Carlotta, had been enormously comforting to us. Every time we were admitted to the hospital, one of them prayed with us almost every day. I wondered what they would think of our decision to create a baby to help save Andy. The Pope had certainly condemned it. I wondered who else cared.

"Are you sure you're OK going through with this?" I asked Paulina. "It's going to be grueling, especially for you. And beyond the physical stuff, we know what the church says about IVF—we're going to be dealing with some negative reactions. Probably from our own family and friends. We can guess which ones already…"

Paulina's eyes flashed. "How can you even ask me that? This is our chance to save Andy and get another baby too! Of course I'm OK with it, I just want to get going as soon as possible." She paused. "I'm sorry if some people aren't happy with our decision, and I know we'll be hearing about it, but it will never make me change my mind."

"But you know we're going to be creating some embryos we'll never be able to use, right? Some may be destroyed in the process. I just want to make sure you're not going to feel we're destroying babies, like the Church claims. Because I don't feel that way—to me, a ball of eight cells in a dish is not the same as a baby. Not until it's implanted, growing, becoming a fetus."

"Andrés, don't worry, I feel the same. I'd never agree to an abortion, but this is different. I don't think we're wrong to try everything possible to cure Andy, including IVF. I may not understand every detail, but I think it's amazing that science has come to this point where it's even an option."

In the next room, Andy woke, crying. Paulina kissed me and went to get him up from his nap. Then she called out from Andy's bedroom. He had another raging fever. We were back in the hospital within hours.

Window sign in our room on 8 East, Children's Hospital Boston.

Chapter Thirteen
Long Days

During our hospitalization in October, Paulina would return to the apartment to sleep while I stayed with Andy. Sometimes we'd switch. Andy didn't sleep much, waking every 20 minutes screaming. I'd change his diaper; sponge his head with a wet towel. I tried to comfort him by rubbing his stomach or holding his hand, *"Aqui estoy contigo, Andy.* I'm here with you. Where does it hurt?"

Sometimes the only thing that calmed him at night was wheeling him in his stroller along the dim, empty corridors. I'd gotten to know another father, named Mohammed, a sad-faced older man from Kuwait. He also strolled his little girl at night, trailing an infusion pump and oxygen tank on wheels. "Say 'Hi,'" he'd tell Samira. "Say 'Hi,'" I'd remind Andy.

Sometimes we'd be drawn to the TV in the lounge, with its late news of international turmoil and the threat of a new Iraq war. We'd position the kids' strollers so they could look at each other, not the TV. Once I asked Mohammed what he did in Kuwait.

He answered in his heavy accent, "I was a one-star general in the army."

"Wow! Did you participate in the Gulf War?" I asked.

He looked at me with dark, serious eyes. "Yes, I was a prisoner of war in 1990."

I probed further. "Where were you kept?"

"Saddam Hussein kept me and my regiment in a series of prison camps in Iraq."

"Let me ask you one more question. Which do you find more difficult: being a prisoner of war or being here with your daughter?"

"To be here taking care of my daughter is worse, no doubt about it," he answered. "When I was a prisoner, I knew the war would end eventually and we'd return to our families. The worst thing that happened to us is that we were forced to clean the prison, and as soon as we finished we were moved to another one to start all over again. But here you see children suffering, you see your own child suffering…"

"I understand," I said. We continued watching the news until our kids' infusion pumps started beeping and we had to return to our rooms.

The $250,000 question

On October 24, Dr. Sung-Yun Pai, a stem cell transplant specialist from Dana-Farber Cancer Institute, visited Andy's room. Since Dana-Farber isn't a pediatric hospital, Children's and Dana-Farber share the transplant program— Andy was one of very few children considered for transplant who *didn't* have cancer. All the inpatient pediatric cancer treatment is housed at Children's. Outpatient care happens at the Jimmy Fund clinic at Dana-Farber, connected to Children's through an elevated, enclosed bridge.

Dr. Pai was a petite Korean-American woman, so youthful-looking that Paulina at first assumed she was a medical student and barely paid attention to her. But I could see the credentials on her badge, and I made Paulina listen as Dr. Pai voiced her concerns. She spoke very softly and I strained to understand her. And she stuck to the facts, showing no emotion as she explained the pros and cons of transplant. Her description seemed heavier on the cons.

"Sometimes, the amount of blood in a newborn's umbilical cord may not be enough for a transplant. The older the recipient, the bigger the blood stem cell transfusion needs to be. Too little blood and the transplant can take too long to attach and replenish and do its job, putting the patient at severe risk. Time is critical," said Dr. Pai.

"Then we need twins or triplets," was Paulina's immediate response.

Dr. Pai told us that given Andy's unstable condition, we might not have enough time to wait for an IVF baby, and that she and her team would start searching US and international bone marrow registries now for compatible donor. We also learned that a successful search for a 100 percent match was rare. She suggested we might have to settle for an 85 or 90 percent match. This confused us even more, since Dr. Orange had made clear that a 100 percent match was essential. Before she left Dr. Pai reiterated that getting Andy strong enough for a transplant was crucial to success.

When I asked her how much the registry search and the transplant would cost, she recommended I visit Dana-Farber's administrative offices across the street from Children's. There I found Monica Kearney, Dana-Farber's pediatric transplant coordinator. After a brief introduction she asked me for a deposit to cover the transplant in advance. Nothing, she asserted, not even beginning the search for a donor, could proceed without a $250,000 deposit. I nodded numbly, told her I needed some time, and left her office.

A quarter of a million dollars. I was pretty sure my insurance wouldn't reimburse much of it, if any. They were already balking on some of Andy's repeat hospitalizations. I'd been away from my job for almost six months. I could sell our apartment instead of renting it out, but then we'd have no income at all. Where would I ever come up with that kind of money?

PGD *setback*

On October 29, Paulina and I drove to Reading for our first appointment at the fertility clinic. It was a rare trip alone, while Andy stayed in the hospital with his nurses. Paulina was in a buoyant mood. "I'm ready for that first hormone shot today!" she said.

Not so fast. First, we both got a full medical check-up and fertility tests. Then Dr. Lee described the protocol in great detail, told us how the scheduling and cycles worked, and gave us a long list of medications Paulina would have to take first. My part was pretty straightforward—merely contributing a semen specimen at the prescribed time. I was cautioned about maintaining a "two-to-four-day abstinence period" before making my donation. *No problem*, I thought. Given our history of nearly 400 nights in the hospital, I was well accustomed to abstinence.

And we made sure Dr. Lee understood we weren't doing just ordinary IVF —we were creating a savior sibling whose umbilical cord could cure our son.

"Is there any way to do gender selection before PGD, since our best option for a disease-free baby is a girl?" Paulina asked.

"Not that I know of," he replied. "But since PGD tests for gender, you'll certainly know which embryos are female." He also told us that the PGD lab set up at Wayne State had to be ready before we started the IVF cycle. We knew Dr. Hughes was still working on it, and it meant more waiting. We drove back to Children's in silence, a little deflated. When we got to our room, Andy's nursing team had posted a cheerful note on our website guestbook:

From: Amy Turgeon, Aimee Glupker, Jenn Shea, Ana Maria Pires, Ruth Goncalvez

Andy, you are the best patient on 8 East! We love that you come and play with us now so Mom and Dad can have some time to themselves. We are so proud of you and love you!

Your nurses on 8 East @ Children's Hospital

The month dragged on, with no news from Dr. Hughes. Andy improved somewhat but he was still unable to tolerate much stomach feeding, only the intravenous nutrition. We were discharged on November 29, having spent another 51 days in the hospital since late summer. When we left, Andy was ecstatic to be outside, staring through the car window and pointing, "¡Nieve! Snow!" His excitement made us laugh and melted the frustration of the last few weeks. He was talking more now and was a little stronger physically, starting to pull himself up against his crib bars. On good days, his laughter made everything worthwhile.

At Christmas, Paulina's parents came up from the tropics of Chiapas to stay for two weeks. The cold weather was shocking to Alfredo and Lupita, as it had been to Paulina. I didn't feel it as much, but she struggled with New England winters—the frigid air, the snowy driving and the logistics of mittens, hats, boots and scarves— it made her even more tired. We hadn't had the relief of a warm Mexican sojourn in eight months.

Predictably, Andy landed back in the hospital on December 27 with a severe colitis flare-up. Though we were always reluctant to use steroids because of their immune-suppressing effects, we tried it, and the response from his inflamed colon was almost immediate. Andy felt so good he gave us a big gift on New Year's Eve. He was standing and cruising around his hospital room holding on to chairs, under the indulgent eyes of Paulina and his grandparents, when suddenly he let go and walked the six steps to his crib. Everyone shouted "Bravo! Good job!" Andy just laughed. When his nurse Aimee entered the room, he proudly showed off his new trick. She was so excited she buzzed the nurses' station and soon they were all crowding the doorway. Andy demonstrated his accomplishment over and over, grinning with each step, until his little legs gave way and he plopped down on his well-diapered bottom. He was 2 ½ years old and finally walking.

One of the cortisone side effects was stimulated appetite, and he was hungry and handling his stomach tube feedings very well. But I was concerned we'd have to confine him to a germ-free bubble to protect his compromised immune system. Dr. Orange organized a special meeting of all Andy's subspecialists in gastroenterology, immunology, infectious disease and dermatology, and they came up with a daily cocktail of 10 medications to protect him in the outside world. The regimen included antibiotics, antivirals, steroids and other anti-inflammatories, plus a gamma globulin infusion every three weeks. The antiviral was specifically intended to fight *cytomegalovirus*, one of Andy's worst intestinal enemies. After another 38 days, we were discharged from the hospital in early February. It scared me to be giving him so many drugs but I had to admit they seemed to be working.

Despite her weariness and worry, Paulina was impatient to start the IVF. I'd been emailing Dr. Hughes every few days since the turn of the New Year, trying to find out whether his lab was ready for us. In late February, he responded:

> *Hi Andrés,*
>
> *We are working on your case, but it's not simple. Knowing the NEMO mutation in your family's DNA is a huge step forward and has allowed us to get started. But, it turns out that there is a "pseudo gene" on the same chromosome, just flanking the true gene that causes the disease. The two genes are 99.99% identical. I have been in contact with Dr. Orange and the Boston team and now am here in San Francisco (3:15 AM – I'm jet lagged), and am meeting today with the person who knows more about this gene than anyone else in the world. We are here for a Genome Conference and have arranged to get together for lunch, to discuss a strategy to get around this problem.*
>
> *If we can't identify the mutation in one cell because of the pseudo gene's presence, we could simply consider identifying embryos that are female and a match to Andy. One-in-eight of your embryos would meet those criteria. We'd prefer to go for the mutation itself, but it may not be possible for anyone to do.*
>
> *I'll get back in touch with you after our strategy sessions here in California.*
>
> *Best Regards,*
>
> *Mark Hughes*

I remembered Jordan Orange mentioning pseudo genes, but I still had to look it up: "Genes that have a structure similar to those of other genes but which are nonfunctioning and can't be expressed. Probably the remnant of a once-functional gene that accumulated mutations…" It would have made me laugh if we hadn't been feeling so desperate.

I busied myself with contacting the Mexican bone marrow registry, since we might need it. I would put out the word to our vast Mexican network of friends and family to get registered. Then it occurred to me that family members might want to get tested for the mutation. We'd never had actual documentation of Andy's NEMO test, or confirmation that Paulina was the carrier. I found the lab that had first tested Andy for the ectodermal dysplasia, GeneDX Laboratory, on the Internet. I called, and ended up talking to Dr. Sherri Bale, their president. I told her our story, and she immediately put me at ease. As a geneticist, she understood everything I said about NEMO. She explained that her lab needed only a buccal swab—a little brush that collected skin cells by lightly scraping across the inside of the cheek—to test for the mutation. She'd mail me a kit and her lab needed only four weeks to get results. I ordered 10 kits, to test Paulina, myself, and give the others to family. They were $300 a piece.

A month later, Dr. Bale sent us the results of their tests confirming Andy's NEMO mutation and Paulina's role as a carrier. We sent kits to our immediate family members so they could be tested too. But after all the kits came back, it was clear that no one else carried the disease. The mutation began with Paulina. She tried to hide her dismay, but I knew she felt guilt and anger despite how impossible it would have been for her to know that in advance. `

On March 3, Dr. Hughes emailed again:

Just to keep you updated: I've spent hours on this—it's not trivial. The guru of this gene is David Nelson of Baylor University and he's both a friend and a former colleague. Even HE is working on this. I don't know what we'll find but we are trying.

Best,

Mark Hughes

Paulina and I each had our own ways of handling the waiting game. She focused on Andy, who was doing so well on the medication cocktail we stayed out of the hospital for weeks at a time. He'd become amazingly energetic, exploring, running and playing every waking minute, learning new words daily, making us laugh. He loved dressing up in costumes. One of his favorites was a black cape and hat and a rubber foil. *"¡Yo soy El Zorillo!"* (Spanish for skunk) he announced, a slightly confused Zorro.

"I'm the happiest mother in the world," Paulina kept saying when we played with toy trucks on our living room floor or walked Andy in the park nearby.

Finally, on March 22, Dr. Hughes called with discouraging news. He was giving up on the NEMO test. We would have to go with testing for gender—female¬—and an HLA match. Even if the girl embryo had NEMO, she would be only a carrier. He'd already called the Fertility Center with the news that we could go ahead.

I had a hard time accepting that failure. Without a valid test, we'd have to eliminate all male embryos, reducing our chances of finding compatibility. But it's all we had.

I turned my focus to figuring out ways to make money. My father and brother found part-time work I could do online for Ekofon, the family company, which helped. I decided to try selling more products than baseball caps and T-shirts on the www.andy.org.mx website. I was looking for things people would use on a regular basis, that I could buy wholesale. I started with personalized phone calling cards at very good rates—the kind people use when calling friends and family overseas—and enlisted some volunteers to sell them. With great enthusiasm, Paulina's aunts Maguis and Ana José were the first volunteers to sign up. I added celebrity autographs, also collected by volunteers, and sold them at auction on eBay in the US and Canada, and on DeRemate in Mexico. The Andy Fund received 30 percent of all sales.

Then my brother, Victor, had a brilliant idea. He suggested we raffle off Paulina's car, the pretty little Mercedes Class A I'd given her back in 2000. It was almost brand-new, still garaged in Mexico City. We registered with the Mexican National Lottery, and with more volunteer help, started selling a limited run of tickets for 450 pesos each. The winner would be announced in December.

Andy turns 3

It was a better spring for Andy, thanks to his meds. He was so active now we ran after him all day. He woke up every morning calling, "Mama, Papa! Sun is up! Want my toys!" Cousin Ivonne returned for another six months. She loved playing with Andy and slept in his room. We welcomed the extra set of hands—Paulina would be going through the stress of starting IVF, and I was spending more time at the computer, trying to find more ways to earn money.

Andy celebrated his third birthday on May 15 at a local family center where he and Paulina had been going for song and story sessions with other little kids and mothers. He loved it, singing along on some of the songs in English. But he was still having trouble eating. After years of intravenous and tube feedings, he didn't know how to swallow food or liquid and he'd gag on anything we introduced on a spoon. Dr. Nurko recommended a feeding therapist, Arden Hill, to help Andy learn to take food orally. Andy enjoyed the group classes where all the children played with food. It took months, but Arden got Andy to drink his Neocate formula in a bottle, then a cup, and we happily abandoned the feeding pump. Introducing solids would prove more of a challenge.

The CIA of NEMO research

In June, Jordan Orange published his NEMO research article in the *Journal of Clinical Investigation*: "Deficient natural killer cell cytotoxicity in patients with IKK-y/NEMO mutations." The study included three patients; Andy was number one. It showed graphs of the patients' flat NK cell response, though one case showed some improvement on IL-2. Too bad it didn't work for Andy. I added the link to the *Journal* on my website, and within days, Mary Kay Richter of the Ectodermal Dysplasia Foundation sent me a message on the website's guestbook.

"Andrés and Paulina, you may find it useful to talk with Sue Lewis, whose son had a successful bone marrow transplant for NEMO a year ago." At last, there was someone else out there! Andy wouldn't be a transplant guinea pig.

I immediately called Sue Lewis. Her 9-year-old son, Nicolas, was the first person with NEMO to be successfully treated. Nic's donor was his 5-year-old brother, a perfect HLA match. She gave me the email address of Dr. Ashish Jain of the National Institutes of Health, who first discovered the NEMO mutation and had recommended the procedure. I remembered Dr. Jain's name as one of the contributors on Dr. Orange's journal article.

Paulina took heart from Sue's story. We shared the details with Dr. Pai, the transplant doctor at Children's/Dana-Farber, who wanted to know the exact chemotherapy doses Nic had received. Sue Lewis put her in contact with all of Nic's doctors. "I feel like we're a central intelligence agency for the medical world," commented Paulina. "They wouldn't know anything about who's doing what with NEMO research or treatment if we weren't gathering all this information and sharing it."

Chapter Fourteen
Assisted Fertility

We got the green light to start the fertility treatments in May, and Paulina happily injected herself with Lupron for six days. This would stimulate her ovaries to produce an abundance of eggs. She travelled to the clinic every day for blood tests and ultrasounds. Then the monitoring center called with instructions to start the follicle-stimulating medication, Gonal-F, triggering the egg-maturing phase. A few days later, I heard cursing coming from our bathroom, where Paulina was giving herself an injection.

"I've been taking only one ampule of the Gonal-F, instead of three! I got it all wrong!" she wailed. We had to abandon the protocol. I knew she felt terrible about it, so I tried to curb my frustration at wasting precious time. We had to wait months for her body to recover, getting back to a normal hormonal base line, before starting all over again.

The second go-ahead from the fertility center came on August 2. Paulina started giving herself the hormone shots again, and this time I checked and double-checked each dosage until she got irritated. Then I teased her about mood swings. Big mistake.

"Go away, I don't need you! Go play on your computer and leave me alone!" she yelled, slamming the door to our room. Ivonne raised a discreet eyebrow and busied herself playing airplanes with Andy.

Somehow we got through the next two weeks, until the daily ultrasound showed 17 eggs were ready. I was so excited I posted the news on our website, which made Paulina angry again. She felt I wasn't respecting our privacy. But the web was my therapy, a window to the outside world. Even if no one read what I wrote, I needed to say it.

Dilemma

Egg retrieval day was also semen specimen day. At the clinic I was escorted to a dimly lit room with an ugly brown couch, a VCR with videos, a toilet and sink—and the kind of "reading material" I used to hide under my mattress as a kid. The nurse handed me a tray with a plastic cup and a marker and told me to make sure I wrote my name on the cup when I finished. "Right, let's have no mix-ups, please." I said. She didn't even smile.

When I returned to the waiting room I was called into the cubicle where Paulina was recovering from the anesthesia. She had shadows under her eyes. "That needle really hurt," she said. Dr. Lee joined us with the news that he'd aspirated 14 eggs. They'd be inseminated in a petri dish that afternoon. Our jobs were done for now.

Paulina stayed in bed for 36 hours with cramps and fever, but the clinic wasn't concerned and recommended a heating pad and Tylenol. Ivonne and I entertained Andy and made sure Paulina rested. The following day the clinic called to say we had seven fertilized eggs.

"Only seven?" Paulina asked.

"I guess the others didn't take," I said. "No blame."

After another 36 hours, the embryologist biopsied each 8-cell cluster and sent the individual cells to Mark Hughes at Wayne State.

Hughes phoned us on August 19, in a conference call with Dr. Lee. Paulina leaned against me, listening. "We've got five male embryos and two females," he told us. "One of the females has a weak compatibility signal, so I can't be sure it's a match. The only strong match is a male."

My heart plunged. It could be a brother who could save Andy—or another dying child. "We can't risk a male, he could have NEMO," I said.

"I know. But there's a test we can do on a fetus after 16 weeks that could help verify if there's a NEMO mutation," he countered.

Paulina, hearing this, was already shaking her head. "No. No way."

"The stakes are too high," I told him. "The whole point of this is to do pre-implantation diagnosis, not fetal diagnosis after an embryo is growing. Abortion isn't an option for us. We need a PGD test."

I saw the pain in Paulina's eyes, and I snatched a passing thought. "Dr. Hughes, do you know Dr. Sherri Bale at GeneDX?"

"Yes, she and I were in graduate school together." He sounded surprised. "Why? How do you know her?"

"Well, she was able to identify NEMO to develop the test kits to check for the mutation in our family. Would it help you to call her and ask how she did it?"

"Yes, of course—I wish I'd known Sherri was working on NEMO! I'll call her right away. If she's already developed the test for the kits, it should only take about six weeks to develop another assay that will work in combination with the HLA test."

"We'll run another IVF cycle as soon as your test is ready," I said, and Paulina nodded.

"It's unlikely the one compatible male embryo would survive a second biopsy when you have the test," said Dr. Lee. "But I'll freeze the remaining embryos, just in case."

After the call Paulina and I held each other for a few moments, swallowing disappointment and wondering how to gather strength for another try. We knew we were facing another long climb up the roller coaster.

NIH *adventure*

While we were waiting to begin another cycle, the National Institutes of Health invited us to Bethesda, Maryland, to be part of a NEMO study. Dr. Ashish Jain, the NEMO expert and Dr. Orange's co-author, was leading the investigation. He was also the one who recommended and supervised Nic Lewis' stem cell transplant. Paulina agreed that we'd cooperate with anything that could lead to more information about treatments and cures.

We traveled to Washington, DC, on September 10 with Ivonne and Andy, where the NIH put us up in a hotel and transported us back and forth to their vast clinical center, a monstrously large brick fortress. We pretended it was a vacation. It had been more than a year since we'd been out of Boston. Andy was thrilled with everything about the trip, wide-eyed at the window of the plane, running aboard the shuttle bus, bouncing on the big bed in the hotel room. The pretense didn't last long. It turned into a grueling three days of researcher interviews, specialist visits and medical tests. The blood draws were especially traumatic. Andy howled and fought the phlebotomist, who wasn't nearly so skilled in finding tiny veins as George, our favorite IV nurse at Children's. It took Ivonne, Paulina and two nurses to hold him down.

But after Ivonne led Andy to a playroom, we spent several hours with Dr. Jain, who knew more about NEMO than anyone on the planet. He was very articulate, patient with our questions, and his explanations were the most complete we'd heard. He told us that out of 14 NEMO cases known to the NIH, Andy was the only one where the mutation was on the gene's fourth exon. Andy had his own rare version of an exceedingly rare disease.

"As you know, NEMO stands for Nuclear Factor Kappa B Essential Modulator, or NFKB, the name of a protein found in the protoplasm of almost all cells," said Dr. Jain. "NEMO is a 'master switch' protein, which regulates signals between the cell membrane and the cell nucleus. If NEMO isn't present, life isn't possible."

Jain stood at the chalkboard and drew a cell. "This master switch protein is in the pathway that activates skin, skeleton, blood vessel, and some organ development as well as other vital signals. For example, the ectodysplasin-A protein encoded in the EDA gene is known to dictate properties of the ectoderm, which is the early developing embryo's last cell layer that becomes skin, hair and teeth. Now, here's something interesting: The EDA gene uses the NEMO pathway to the nucleus to 'switch on' the ectoderm properties. Your son has ectodermal dysplasia because the pathway of the EDA gene is blocked or finds a different route on the mutated fourth exon of the NEMO gene. Andy's ectodermal dysplasia—his lack of sweat glands, his pointed teeth and sparse hair—might look like other forms of ED, but his mutation is fundamentally different. And deadly. There's no immune deficiency in those other types."

"And there's no other case we know of with NEMO and ulcerative colitis," he continued. "Ulcerative colitis is caused by different conditions, one of which may be regulated by another gene, 'NOD2.' So the NOD2 gene also may be encountering a blocked pathway when trying to send signals to the cell nucleus."

"I've been reading about gene therapy," I told Jain. "Can't we just supply the missing proteins where they're needed?"

"For most diseases, genetic therapy is still theoretical," he replied. "To date, there's no way to know the amount of NFKB protein needed, or how to deliver it exactly where it needs to go to work. Only a matched blood stem cell transplant from umbilical cord blood or bone marrow could substitute the faulty NEMO gene, and *only* in blood cells. We know blood cells are produced by blood stem cells in the bone marrow. If Andy's mutated blood stem cells are replaced with cells that carry a complete version of NEMO, the pathway problem is fixed. The bone marrow transplant wouldn't fix the NEMO mutation in other types of cells, like the ectoderm, but the problems caused by the signals on these tissues are not terminal."

He paused. "So that's why, even though it won't replace anything but the blood cell genes, a bone marrow transplant can correct his worst symptoms—those affecting his immune response. My only caution is that the transplant procedure carries the risk of organ damage, or worse, from the chemotherapy that will destroy his immune system before the transplant."

We left the meeting with our brains nearly bursting. We treated Andy to a few hours at the National Air and Space Museum, and crashed in our hotel with a take-out dinner. Andy drank his formula and chattered about airplanes and rockets and "the pilots in space" until he fell asleep.

For the next few days we met with dozens of specialists: immunology, dermatology, audiology, gastroenterology, transplantation, infectious disease, nutrition and dentistry. They examined every aspect of Andy's symptoms and offered some insights on new feeding formulas, Andy's problem teeth and his current medications. They also extended their scrutiny to Paulina, as a NEMO carrier. When Andy was first diagnosed with ectodermal dysplasia, she'd mentioned to a Children's dermatologist that she also had a few symptomatic dry skin patches. Now she gamely went off to the dermatology clinic to have her skin, hair and teeth analyzed by a group of uniformed military doctors, knowing it might provide clues to diagnose another X-linked carrier. She returned an hour later, her cheeks flaming.

"There were 20 of them, all there to look at the skin on my legs! They formed a line!" she said to Ivonne. "You should have come with me—some of them must have been single."

I was annoyed. "Did you charge them admission?"

Paulina laughed at me.

Our last interview was with Dr. Horwitz, a bone marrow transplant specialist who was exploring his theory that transplants for immune deficiencies should be different than those for cancer. "The standard procedure to get rid of blood malignancies like leukemia uses chemotherapy to destroy *all* the patient's bone marrow, before transfusing in the new healthy blood stem cells from donor marrow. But immune deficiencies don't include malignancies, so patients like Andy might be better candidates for a 'mini-transplant' with far less toxic doses of chemo."

He told us that umbilical cord cells had never been tried in such cases before, but he was working on an NIH protocol to offer cord blood transplants to immune-deficient patients. It would be ready in a year, and might be an option for Andy. He was also fascinated by our IVF and PGD experiences, because NIH researchers were prohibited by federal law from working with embryonic stem cells or anything to do with embryos. He was acquainted with our PGD champion, Dr. Hughes, who had worked at the NIH and left to work in privately funded research for that reason. Dr. Horwitz encouraged us to keep trying for a compatible embryo while also pursuing public donor registries.

We had the remainder of the week to explore Washington's national sites and treasures. Everywhere we went people stared at Andy—he was so small and his face was so swollen from the steroids. Fortunately he didn't notice. We returned to Boston with a lot to think about.

IVF Cycle 3

By the end of September the fertility clinic wanted to begin another cycle. Dr. Hughes was ready to try his new PGD assay.

So Paulina started her injections, reporting daily to the clinic for blood tests and ultrasounds, and by October 9 she was ready for egg retrieval. This time, we got a paltry eight eggs. After I did my part in the room with the brown couch and joined Paulina in the recovery room, we heard another couple rejoicing on the other side of the curtained cubicle, "Twenty-two eggs!"

Paulina, pale and nauseated from the knock-out drugs, was sipping ginger ale. "We have only eight. Something must be wrong with me," she whispered.

"We need only one, the right one," I answered. But of the eight eggs, only four fertilized, and when we called Dr. Hughes a few days later he told us, "I need at least five cells from five embryos to run the test. Better to freeze these four, then run another cycle and let me test all of them at once."

Another roller coaster dive. Paulina's mood was bitter.

"Do you want to go through another cycle?" I asked her. "Do you feel up to it? I don't like you taking all these hormones—it's too hard on your body, on your emotions."

"I could go through it a hundred times if I knew it would work. But I'm just not sure," she answered. "Maybe while Andy's doing well on the medications we should postpone the transplant and just enjoy him. Take him back to Mexico so he'll get to know all his family. Maybe this is in God's hands."

"I think we should try one more time, then that's it," I countered. "If it doesn't work, if we can't find a compatible girl, we stop and work harder to search the donor registries. One more try."

"OK. We only have enough money for one more try, anyway." As if she needed to reminded me.

Preschool

While we waited for Paulina's body to recover, we comforted ourselves by watching Andy's progress. He spent his September check-up telling Batman stories, to Dr. Nurko's delight. Nurko wanted to wean Andy off the heavy prednisone by decreasing the dose on alternate days. Even though his compromised immune system was somewhat at risk, Andy was cleared to attend a half-day preschool. The Phineas Lawrence School in Waltham offered special education services, including physical, occupational, motor skills and speech/language therapies. We were amazed that all this was available—in Mexico, only the poorest families used public schools. He'd be in a very small classroom with just a few other children with special needs, in order to limit his exposure to the germs and bugs most kids could take in stride. We were happy to learn that the school nurse, Carole Ferguson, had been a nurse practitioner at Children's and understood all Andy's issues.

Though we'd brought an enthusiastic Andy to visit the school the previous week, we were prepared for some clinging and tears on his first day, October 21. But he was so excited he ran into the classroom without a backward glance. Despite all he'd been through, or maybe because of it, Andy seemed unafraid of anyone or anything at that moment. We were the ones standing damp-eyed in the hallway of the Lawrence School.

Chapter Fifteen
Adrenaline Crises

Our financial situation made me sleepless. The car raffle ticket sales brought in some income, but it was barely enough to cover Andy's formula and medication cocktail. At the moment, we were waiting for confirmation of our legal immigration status and our medical insurance coverage was pending. The IVF costs were also uninsured, even though the clinic gave us free Lupron and Gonal medication left over from other couples' successful procedures.

I'd found some Mexican contacts in New York City and I decided to spend a few days there selling the Andy Fund phone calling cards. Since Andy seemed stable, Paulina was between cycles and Cousin Ivonne was still with us, it seemed safe to leave. I took the bus down from Boston, and stayed in the empty apartment of one of my brother's friends.

It had been turning into a productive trip, when, two days later, my cell phone rang at 6:30 a.m. Paulina's voice was calm, but she said she and Ivonne were taking Andy to the Children's Emergency Department. He'd been up all night with diarrhea and vomiting.

"I'll head home right away."

"No, no, everything's under control, go ahead with your appointments."

Ivonne called an hour later. "We're at the hospital now and Paulina says, on second thought, come home as soon as possible."

While I was tossing things into my overnight bag to head to Port Authority, Paulina called again. This time she sounded frantic. "They're telling me there's something wrong with his blood pressure and heartbeat! I'm scared, and I'm not sure I'm telling them what they need to know in English. Can you find Dr. Orange and ask him to come right away?" Jordan Orange knew as much about Andy's case as anyone.

My hands shook as I called the hospital and had Jordan paged. He picked up immediately. "Jordan, please, we need your help—Andy's in some sort of crisis in the ER!" I told him.

"I'm on my way, I'll be there in a few minutes," he answered.

Later, Paulina reached me on the bus. Her voice was hoarse as she described how Dr. Orange had calmed the emergency room chaos and given the team Andy's critical information. Andy was now stabilized in the ICU. It was the most agonizingly slow bus ride I'd ever taken, and after calling my brother in Mexico to let the family know what was happening, I prayed the whole way. When I finally got to the hospital, I found Paulina in the ICU, her eyes red-rimmed. We hugged each other long and hard.

"I'm so sorry I wasn't here—I'll never leave you alone like that again," I told her.

Andy was hooked up to a half-dozen monitors. He was conscious but weak, and when he tried to greet me he couldn't speak.

"It's OK, Andy, your eyes tell me a lot. Just rest, I'm here."

But as soon as he gained a little strength, he smiled for his nurses and made a few observations. *"Papá, uno de mis doctores es pelón como tú.* One of my doctors is bald like you. And another one has red lips like a clown."

It took another day to figure out what was going on. Andy had a second episode while in the ICU, flailing violently, staring blindly at the ceiling, screaming that he wanted to leave, *"Ya vámonos, Ya vámonos!"*

His monitors set off a "code-blue" emergency and his room filled with doctors and nurses. Paulina was so terrified she couldn't move. I held Andy tightly while a doctor gave him a tranquilizer, then another dose of steroids. Gradually, he fell asleep.

When I called my father to update him later that evening, my voice broke and I started to cry. "Wait, really, he's fine now, I just need to calm down—AHHH! I don't know why I can't stop crying." I pressed my fingers against my eyes, struggling to gain control, until my dad started crying, too. *Great, the two of us,* I thought.

His doctors guessed a blood infection—septic shock—contributed to adrenal failure, which causes all vital functions start to shut down. The adrenal glands produce cortisol, a natural steroid, to regulate pulse, blood pressure, blood sugar and electrolyte levels and temperature. When they fail, so do vital signs.

A blood test showed not a blood infection, but a rotavirus infection in his stomach. No surprise.

Dr. Orange elaborated, "Adrenal failure happens sometimes with people on steroids. The glands aren't producing enough cortisol to regulate blood pressure and blood sugar, etc.—probably because the gland that directs cortisol production, the hypothalamus, is tricked by the medication cortisone into not producing more. Andy's been taking prednisone for months, so the hypothalamus isn't sending signals to produce cortisol. The adrenals can even become smaller over time when they're not activated. We'll have to watch Andy for any signs of stress like an infection or dehydration or fatigue, and increase his steroids until the stress is controlled. Even if it also increases his immunosuppression."

I began to despair that we'd ever wean him off the prednisone. How long would we be trapped in this vicious cycle?

After four days in the ICU, we went home. Andy was happy to return to preschool, but it was hard to let him out of our sight. We instructed his teacher, Shannon, in what to be alert for, and wondered if we'd ever be able to relax. Within weeks another stomach infection landed us back in the hospital. Andy had another "code blue," hallucinating and babbling nonsense, then slowly losing consciousness. Again, the doctors searched for a vein while Andy became nearly comatose. Finally they got an IV into his foot and administered the stress steroids. My own adrenaline was in overdrive until Andy stabilized.

It turned into another 10-day inpatient stay. After so many years of this Andy was old enough to start asking, "Why?" So one morning I said to him, "Do you know why your stomach hurts sometimes?"

"Mmm, no," he answered, looking into my eyes for a response.

"Well, turns out you have some little fish in your stomach that are not behaving. They're so tiny you can't see them, except with special machines like X-rays. The little fish try to keep your stomach healthy but they don't know how to do it."

He nodded, he was getting interested.

"It's very important that you feed your fish in your stomach because they are very hungry," I told him. "And sometimes they need medicine to behave."

"Well, that's OK. I have lots of medicine," he answered.

Financial relief

In the middle of that hospitalization I got wonderful news. Our insurance company accepted our petition to keep covering Andy's hospitalization costs. We desperately needed it if we were in for another period of crisis trips to the Emergency Department. I was encouraged enough to wonder if there might be a way also to get help with the IVF expenses—the clinic had asked for our account to be settled in full and the next cycle prepaid before starting again. I wrote to the clinic director, Dr. Vito Cardone, explaining our desperate situation and asking for a discount. To my great joy, he agreed.

We moved to an apartment in Auburndale, a village of Newton, Massachusetts, that lies along the banks of the Charles River. The apartment had two rooms, two bathrooms and a very small kitchen. It was a shorter drive to the hospital.

Transplant review

I decided we should meet again with Dr. Pai, the bone marrow transplant specialist. Now that our health insurance seemed on track, we wanted to follow her initial recommendation to pursue an unrelated donor from a registry even as we were continuing our IVF efforts.

Dr. Pai was impressed with Andy's improved health in the year since she'd first consulted with us, but understood why his current adrenal suppression issues were increasing our urgency.

In her neutral way, she voiced concern that using umbilical cord blood might not work as well as a transplant of mature bone marrow. Cord blood stem cells, fresh from the womb, risked being too "naïve," their immune power not fully developed. She recommended continuing the bone marrow registry search and told us she thought she had around 20 possible donors for Andy. I was skeptical, since her views of HLA compatibility were different from everything else we'd been told about needing a 100 percent match.

She also reviewed the transplant risks for us:

• Chemotherapy to kill the immune system is dangerously toxic to the body, and some people can't recover from it.

• Serious infection is a possibility after chemo, when the new immune system isn't fully functional.

• There's a danger of fatal graft-versus-host disease, in which the donor's cells reject the body they're introduced to.

Further, there was no guarantee that even a successful transplant would cure Andy's colitis, a related but separate health issue. He might be steroid-dependent forever. Finally, she said she needed a full commitment from us to follow through on confirming possible donors. We couldn't back out once she identified a match.

Dr. Pai's insistence on giving us the full dose of scary facts was hard to absorb. And we weren't ready to commit to an unrelated donor if she found one. So we thanked her for her time, told her we had one more IVF cycle to try, and left. She and her registry recommendation were part of a back-up plan, and right now we just wanted to focus on Plan A, another IVF cycle.

Cycle 4

The Christmas holidays brought Paulina's parents for a visit. We all kept close watch on Andy. He had an upper respiratory infection, but it seemed to bother us more than him. He now wore a medical alert bracelet, and we carried "stress dose" steroid medication at all times, but he was a mostly happy and engaged little boy. He was steadily becoming bilingual, especially at school, and called us "Dad" and "Mom" when he spoke English. His English phrase of choice was, "Will you play airplanes with me?" His grandparents were only too happy to comply. He also loved watching videos—anything by Disney—and "The Wizard of Oz" was his favorite movie. On Christmas Eve he asked Paulina, "Mama, has the Baby Oz arrived yet?"

Paulina rolled her eyes, "It's the Baby Jesus!"

And when Alfredo and Lupita ended their visit and said good-bye, he begged, "Stay with me, Grandma."

She replied, "But if I did, who will take care of Grandpa?"

"Well, his mother of course," Andy answered.

I missed my own parents and the rest of my family. My father emailed a long, eloquent letter to Andy on New Year's Eve, a message so loving it brought tears, and at the same time, lifted my spirits. I read it to Andy when I put him to bed.

"My beloved and admired Andy," it began.

> *"From you we have learned so much. You will not remember all the suffering you've faced since you were born, but all of us will remember that during those difficult moments we gave our best, out of love, following the example of your brave and determined parents. Andrés and Paulina have given the best of themselves at every level... demonstrating that they know how to be who they really are. All of us follow slightly behind. You have a very special destiny, and as you face what's ahead you will find your own answers, armed with the enormous advantage that you are so loved. Love us back. And the force of your own love will give you the clues to resolve everything that is presented to you..."*
>
> *Your Grandfather,*
>
> *Victor E. Treviño*

Paulina was being monitored by the clinic and they told her she was ready to begin her injections for our next—and final—IVF cycle, January 1. It took the last of our car raffle money to pay for it. We'd selected the winning ticket on Christmas Eve—Paulina's Mercedes went to a lucky man in Mexico City. She admitted feeling sad over losing her nice car, just as she had when we rented out our beautiful apartment and packed away all our belongings, but the sadness passed quickly. "It's funny, but those material things don't mean as much any more. I think I'm becoming a minimalist."

She woke up excited each morning for the next 14 days, driving to the clinic in ice and snow for blood tests, ultrasounds and temperature readings and eagerly injecting herself every afternoon. "This is going to be the one, I can feel it. You'll see."

"It's a good way to start the New Year," I answered, wanting to believe it.

On January 13, 2003, Paulina wrote on Andy's website,

Hola!

I'm writing to ask you all to say a Hail Mary, Our Father or whatever you believe works best, tomorrow at 11:45 EST. That's when we'll be doing our last in vitro fertilization attempt to find a compatible brother or sister for the bone marrow transplant Andy so desperately needs. Maybe if we all pray to God at the same time he will listen! I really appreciate it.

Love,

Paulina

Russian Roulette

Paulina was shivering when she got into the car for our trip to the clinic, and it snowed on the way. But this time our specialist, Dr. Ian Hardy, retrieved 16 eggs.

"Yes, this is going to be the good one!" Paulina said, followed by "What went wrong?" when, a day later, they told us only four eggs fertilized. I secretly wondered if it was my fault. Maybe my contribution wasn't good enough? The blastomere biopsies travelled to Dr. Hughes in Michigan.

When Dr. Hughes and Dr. Hardy conference-called us on Sunday, January 19, I knew instantly from their voices the news wasn't good. I couldn't look at my wife's face when Mark Hughes said; "We tried the new NEMO test on all the cells from the new batch as well as those from the thawed embryos. Unfortunately, the test failed again. The pseudo gene is still preventing me from getting a clear enough signal from that single cell. The only HLA compatibles I found are two males and I don't know if they have NEMO. I'm very sorry."

And Dr. Hardy said, "If you want to go ahead with the transfer, I recommend implanting both embryos to increase your chance of becoming pregnant. I know it's difficult, but you need to make a decision right now. The thawed embryos can't be refrozen—implantation can't wait."

"What do we do?" I asked Paulina.

"If I get pregnant and the amnio test shows the baby has NEMO, I'm not having an abortion," she said.

"I know, I know," I answered. "I just wish we had more time to think about this. We'll either fix the problem or make it two or even three times worse. This is like Russian roulette!"

"We just have to have faith," she answered. "Faith in the positive, 50 percent chance."

So we drove to the clinic that afternoon, which was open even on Sunday. The two HLA compatible embryos were implanted in Paulina. I sat with Andy in the waiting room, two thoughts alternating in my brain, *God must know what he wants to send us* and *What are we doing?!*

Dr. Lee, the embryologist, walked past us in the hallway. He returned with a marker and a latex glove that he blew up like a balloon, drew a face on, and handed to Andy, who was charmed.

"Will I get a baby brother?" my son asked me. He'd been listening.

Paulina and I didn't exchange a word on the way home.

The next week was tense. Images of Andy's worst moments filled my thoughts. Paulina was withdrawn, resting and praying as I paced and panicked.

Then I received a call from Monica Kearney, the stem cell transplant coordinator from Children's Hospital/Dana-Farber Medical Center. "Mr. Treviño, we've found a registry match for your son!"

"What? Are you sure? We didn't give the go-ahead yet, but that's wonderful news!"

"The National Bone Marrow Donor Program is going to contact your donor. I just wanted to let you know," she continued.

"This is amazing! Where did they find the donor?"

"That's information I can't give you, but Dr. Pai will get back to you with more details. We'll be receiving a blood sample from the donor tomorrow."

I hung up and shouted, "Paulina, the registry found a donor! A full match!"

She appeared in the bedroom door, smiling. "Maybe our prayers are finally being answered," she said.

I was so excited I immediately emailed the news to Jordan Orange. He responded that if Paulina's pregnancy didn't take, an unrelated matched donor was a reasonable alternative for transplant. He cautioned that the evaluations for donors couldn't cover all compatibilities, and there was never a full substitute for an HLA-identical sibling. "Nevertheless," he wrote, "this is good news and a unique opportunity for Andy."

I called my parents in Mexico City to give them the news. There had just been another moderate earthquake there, which they interpreted as a sign that things were shaking up for the better.

Early in the morning of January 24, Paulina went to the clinic for her pregnancy test, and then returned home to wait for the monitoring center's call. At noon, the phone rang.

"I'm so sorry to tell you—the pregnancy test was negative."

As crushed as we both felt, Paulina confessed she'd been deeply uneasy about the possibility of carrying another terminally-ill baby. "At least I can thank God for not sending us that again." And I agreed.

Donor hide and seek

And now we had to move forward again. I alerted Dr. Orange and Dr. Pai about the failed pregnancy. Now what? The choice we faced was grim; keeping Andy on a high-risk medication cocktail with the inevitable dire consequences; or proceeding with an unrelated donor transplant, with its own risks of rejection and failure. Dr. Pai replied that she was still reviewing the information from the potential donor, but in February she would like to start the pre-transplant work-up on Andy, which would take several weeks. Then we could decide on the exact timing of the transplant.

She also mentioned she had applied to the local Make-a-Wish chapter on Andy's behalf, in case we'd like a special trip or experience before he was hospitalized. The Make-a-Wish Foundation is a wonderful organization that gives kids with life-threatening illness a chance to have a dream come true. The child's choice could be almost any longed-for experience, like being a fireman or ballerina for a day, meeting a famous athlete or visiting a cherished destination. I couldn't wait to tell Andy, who knew instantly what he wanted. It eased our sore hearts a bit when Tim McGowan, a Boston Make-a-Wish representative, visited us at the apartment a few days later. Andy had an attack of shyness, and hid behind my legs when Tim asked him what he wished for. He looked up at me and whispered in Spanish, "Papa, you tell him."

"No, Andy, you have to speak up and say what your wish is."

"I want to go to Disney," he whispered.

"What? We can't hear you."

"Disney!" he shouted, still gripping my knees but breaking into a wide grin.

A week later Andy had another adrenal episode. It followed the same pattern: Nurko had recently reduced the prednisone, the colitis flared, and the pain sent Andy into screaming incoherence, then adrenal shock. We were at home, and the crisis came on so fast we had no time to call 911 or get him to the Emergency Department. While I held his barely-conscious body, Paulina injected Andy with the stress-dose steroids we carried at all times. Slowly he came back to us. I called our endocrinologist at Children's to let him know we'd used the shot. Andy took a nap. He woke later as if nothing had happened, happily trotting through the apartment with his arms spread saying, "Look, I'm an airplane!" Paulina and I had collapsed on the couch, our nerves still twitching.

"We can't keep doing this," I said. "The medications are going to kill him. I think we have to go ahead with the transplant from the donor registry."

She sighed. "It still scares me. There's so many ways it could go wrong. But I know you've researched every angle, and if you think it's the best way, I trust you."

The next day I spelled out my hopes, questions and concerns in a long email to Dr. Pai. Her reply was much shorter.

From: Pai, Sung-Yun, MD

Sent: Sat 2/1/2003 9:07 a.m.

To: Andrés Treviño

Cc: Paulina Treviño

When I met with you last, I was under the impression that there was a "full match." One of the physicians told me that she thought it was of all 10 antigens, but she wasn't sure. Sometimes when people say "full match" they only mean 6 antigens, which was all we used to type for in the past. In any case, I have been looking at the typing myself, and from what I have seen so far the match is not 10/10, which carries a higher risk of graft vs. host disease.

This whole endeavor is about weighing odds. But in this case the odds are not precise, and more importantly, all the numbers and statistics and guesses in the world will not tell us what exactly will happen to Andy himself. Please let me get the rest of the information I need (in hard copy so I know the facts for sure) and let's meet again. The most important thing is that Andy has been doing well with his current regimen and there is no rush right now. So I want you both to have adequate time to make a decision you can feel comfortable with. I think too, that even after we have met, perhaps your whole family needs some time away to have some perspective. I will contact you soon.

Sincerely,

Sung-Yun Pai

I was dumbfounded. "I can't believe this—it's not a full match after all! And how can she say there's no rush when she knows Andy's having these adrenal episodes? "

Paulina was furious. "How can they do this? They told us *we* had to make a commitment, with no turning back! But they can make this kind of mistake? How can *they* just toy with us like that?" Then she wept.

My response was to pursue a Mexican bone marrow donor with greater urgency. I spent a futile week trying to convince the country's premier bone marrow bank in Mexico City to be open to receiving more registrants—especially all our family members and friends who wanted to help. They had only 3,000 samples in their bank —a search with any statistical chance of a match requires at least a million. Thinking I was helping to solve an obvious problem, I lined up reputable blood laboratories in areas of the country where we knew people. These labs readily agreed to facilitate gathering and sending blood samples to the registry bank. But Dr. Clara Gorodesky, the volatile bank director, was furious at my interference. "We have the best lab in Mexico— state of the art—we don't need any outside help!" She insisted that anyone who wanted to register could come in person to her lab. That wouldn't help Paulina's family in Chiapas or our friends in Monterrey who'd have to fly to the capital. No wonder the registry was so small. Dr. Gorodesky made it clear she wasn't interested in growing the registry, only in presiding over a small boutique enterprise. "We're the best immunology lab in Mexico," she kept shouting.

I gave up in utter frustration, turning instead to the US registry. After all, it included more people of Mexican descent than the one representing all of Mexico. On the Internet, I found a lab which could provide a way for friends and family who hadn't yet been tested for compatibility to join the registry, involving a few drops of blood on filter paper, mailed to the US. But no one was a full match.

So we were back at square one. Somehow, we had to find a way to do another IVF cycle, and get lucky.

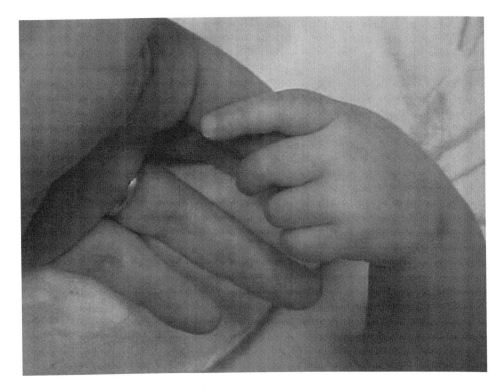

Andy with Andrés at Children's Hospital, 2003.

Chapter Sixteen
Puzzle Pieces

As soon as I emailed Mark Hughes to let him know we were thinking of trying IVF/PGD again, he replied with good news.

> *Regarding the NEMO test: we solved it already. The entire thing works together now. Hopefully, that puts a smile on your face!*

I couldn't tell him that I wasn't fully convinced, that he'd gotten our hopes up too many times before. He also informed me that Wayne State University wouldn't cover the PGD expenses any more, so if we proceeded we'd have to pay at least his break-even expenses.

But we had to go ahead.

Sperm sorting for a girl

On March 20, we went to our follow-up appointment at The Fertility Center of New England to review the failed attempts and our remaining options. This time, we met with Dr. Vito Cardone, the clinic director, and I was glad to have the opportunity to thank him for the discount he'd given us on the previous cycles.

After Paulina's physical exam, we sat with Dr. Cardone in his office. Even though I assumed he was familiar with our case, I reviewed the NEMO diagnosis, Andy's prognosis and Dr. Hughes' struggles with the PGD test.

Paulina interrupted. "Dr. Cardone, we've been told by Dr. Lee that there's no known way to select for a boy or girl before fertilization. Is that true? I know that sperm can be sorted for gender in cattle breeding—that's what my father does on his ranch. Why can't it be done for humans?"

Dr. Cardone raised his eyebrows. "Well, yes, there is a way to do pre-fertilization gender selection, or at least increase the odds. And since this NEMO condition you're telling me about is an X-linked condition, you'd benefit from getting a girl. As a matter of fact, I know there's a company in Virginia that's doing a trial on sperm sorting right now. Wait while I look this up," and he spun his Rolodex. "Here it is, Microsort. Call them and ask about sperm sorting." He handed me a card with a phone number.

I exchanged a glance with Paulina. She looked as stunned as I felt. This odds–altering development threw open a new door. We knew we had to walk through it, whatever the cost.

"Great!" I said to Dr. Cardone. "You may have us in here for another IVF cycle soon. Thank you!"

On the way home from Reading, Paulina burst out angrily, "It's incredible that these doctors never seem to be able to put two and two together or share any information! It's there in our record we have an X-linked condition. They *know* we need a girl. Why couldn't they tell us about sperm sorting when we first started? Think of all the time we've wasted, the chances we've missed!"

I was too busy dialing the Microsort number in Virginia to answer.

Microsort directed me to their website to fill out registration forms. I faxed them out the next day. The website described their technology: Because female sperm tends to be larger than male, a cell measuring technique called flow cytometry is used to identify and separate the larger sperm cells. A fluorescent dye with DNA probes is introduced to the sample of presumed female cells. The dye attaches to the cells' chromosomes, turning pink in X chromosomes and green in Y. Under a microscope, the sample can be reviewed for relative gender purity—the pinker it is, the more X chromosomes there are, the more female sperm. *Wow!* I thought. *We're in business!*

PGD Back-up

In the same Internet search, I found a pre-implantation genetic diagnosis clinic in Chicago, the Reproductive Genetics Institute, RGI. Figuring an alternative to Dr. Hughes couldn't hurt, I called them. At my request, RGI set up a phone consult with a genetic counselor, Renee Genovese, who'd never heard of NEMO but sounded very interested in our history of failed PGD tests.

"Let me be more specific: We need to perform PGD related to the nuclear factor kappa b essential modifier gene mutation, L153R NEMO and human leukocyte antigen-HLA identification." I said, reading from my notes.

"I'll talk to our director, Dr. Verlinsky, and get back to you," Renee replied. "Maybe we can help."

Soon we were filling out genetics forms for RGI, requesting more blood samples from relatives, and cross-checking the DNA information with GeneDx, the company who had done the previous family analysis. Renee Genovese explained that, unlike Dr. Hughes' lab, RGI did two types of PGD—polar body removal as well as the blastomere biopsy—to increase the amount of genetic information. I'd never heard of polar bodies, but it sounded as though they could contribute to a more thorough test, and I was all for it. I learned that polar bodies are by-products of the division of the mature egg. Before fertilization, the egg discards the first polar body. It can be removed and tested for its chromosome complement or to identify an abnormal gene. At the penetration of the egg by the sperm, but prior to the joining of the sperm's and egg's genetic material, the egg undergoes another cell division, producing two unequally sized cells. The larger cell will join with the sperm's genetic material to create the pre-embryo, and the smaller is the second polar body, and it is also cast off. The polar bodies have no known function except to assist in cell division. But they contain PGD gold.

Renee told us they were going ahead and setting up the lab to do the NEMO test, and thought they had a solution to the pseudo-gene problem that had stumped Mark Hughes and Sherri Bale.

In the meantime, my request to participate in Microsort's sperm-sorting trial was denied—we didn't qualify as having an X-linked condition.

"This just can't be!" I said to Paulina in exasperation.

"Obviously, they'd never heard of NEMO. Talk to someone else."

"I just never thought I'd be negotiating with anyone over my sperm…"

I sent a letter of protest to the Microsort CEO, accompanied by recommendations from Dr. Geha and Dr. Orange of Children's Hospital and Dr. Jain of the NIH. I explained once again what we were up against—I could recite the NEMO story in my sleep.

It worked, they agreed to take me. And when they sent a confirming letter, they referred us to Reproductive Genetics Institute, RGI, in Chicago, for the PGD test; they actually had their own Microsort collaborator there.

"That's not a coincidence—that's a sign!" said Paulina

They also agreed to coordinate the procedure with Dr. Cardone at The Fertility Center of New England, where they'd send the sorted, frozen sperm after I made the deposit in Virginia.

"Yes!" said Paulina. "Now we're getting somewhere!" She put her arms around me. "You'll have to go and do that part without me. You've already moved mountains for us. After that, it will be my turn to do the work and I have a feeling it's going to be successful. So many signs are working for us! We'll get our little girl."

Last Try

In late April, Andy broke his leg simply jumping off a step in the playground and his leg was in a cast for weeks. The steroids were weakening his bones.

We embarked on the final cycle. Between discounts from all of the organizations dealing with us, a frenzied round of Andy Fund calling card sales, and loans from our parents, we were just barely able to afford it.

On May 28, I took a morning flight from Boston to Virginia. The ground below was a brilliant green, and I could see masses of pink and white flowering trees as I landed in Fairfax. A huge sign greets visitors at the airport:

VIRGINIA IS FOR LOVERS

At Microsort's affiliate, the Genetics and IVF Institute clinic, I went through the familiar sperm deposit routine, then took a cab back to the airport. I was back home in Auburndale by dinnertime, wondering if my sperm were traumatized in their journey through the land of pink fluorescent flow cytometry.

Paulina started her hormone injections on June 11. She was in a good mood, happy that Carolina, another one of her inexhaustible supply of unmarried cousins, was coming for a few months. She'd have a childhood friend for girl talk, plus help with Andy.

That night a soft breeze stirred the bedroom curtains and we could hear insects humming and frogs peeping in a neighboring park. The whole world around us was buzzing with fecundity. "This is really my season, my climate," murmured Paulina. "My body feels more relaxed—happier—than it has in 10 months." I held her close, but carefully.

A week later, her daily ultrasounds were showing nine eggs in one ovary and eight in the other. In another seven days, the total egg count was 20. On June 19, my frozen, pink, X-sorted sperm travelled via courier from Fairfax, Virginia, to Reading, Massachusetts. *Go, girls!* I thought.

Egg retrieval day was June 25. At the clinic Dr. Cardone, using an ultrasound probe and an aspiration needle, extracted 27 beautiful eggs. "Twenty-seven!" I told Paulina in the recovery room.

"Twenty-seven?" she repeated groggily. "Don't get too excited, it only matters how many fertilize."

That afternoon, Dr. Lee, the fertility center embryologist, joined by a specialist from RGI, removed the first polar bodies from each egg, and couriered the cells to Chicago where the NEMO and HLA tests were waiting. Then, instead of simply mixing the eggs and sperm, Dr. Lee meticulously fertilized the eggs under a microscope using intracytoplasmic injection—a technique involving inserting a single (and, I imagined, stunned) X-sorted sperm into each egg.

Our luck held. Two days later the monitoring center called with the news that 21 eggs had successfully fertilized. We danced around the room, shouting, "Lucky 21!"

In three days, the blastomeres were ready. At the fertility clinic, the RGI embryologist removed one cell from each cluster, carefully labeled them, and hand-carried them to Chicago. The 21 early embryos, full of secrets to be revealed, remained in an incubator in Reading.

Numbers 12 and 26

Then came the morning of June 30 and the call we'd been waiting for. Paulina and I both felt paralyzed, but I managed to pick up the phone. Renee Genovese said, "Mr. Treviño? Here are the results: We analyzed 18 polar bodies and 18 blastomeres—the rest didn't give us strong enough signals to measure. We found nine females, five males and five gender inconclusives. We found three HLA matches, six NEMO mutation carriers and eight non-mutation carriers, with inconclusives among those categories also."

"Yes, yes, but what's the bottom line?!" I tried to keep my voice down. Paulina was leaning against the wall of the kitchen, and slowly slid down to sit on the floor at my feet, her eyes squeezed shut.

"We recommend transferring two embryos, identified as number 12 and number 26. Number 12 is a female HLA match and NEMO mutation carrier. Number 26 is also a female HLA match, and a non-mutation carrier. Good luck!"

We left Andy at home with Carolina, and sped to Reading. At the fertility clinic, Dr. Hardy led Paulina to a small, dim room and for the first time, I was allowed to accompany her. Dr. Hardy already had embryos 12 and 26 loaded in a flexible catheter and quickly transferred them to Paulina's waiting womb. Then he left us alone. For an hour and a half I played classical music

—Bach¬—and massaged Paulina's feet as she relaxed and drifted in and out of sleep. After, as we'd decided, I checked her into a Marriott near our apartment so she could stay off her feet for another 24 hours.

"Order room service if you need anything," I told her. "Try not to get up."

Paulina nodded sleepily from the middle of the huge bed. "I promise."

That night I put Andy to bed, got into bed myself, and mused about the mystery of conception. Despite all the highly controlled technology involved in what we'd just gone through, whether an embryo attached or not was up to an ancient force: Fate. Then I fell asleep.

The Test

We had to wait 10 days for a pregnancy test. I tried to get Paulina to rest and relax as much as possible. Her cousin Carolina was still with us, and her grandmother, Margot, arrived, so she had no excuses. Margot began cooking as soon as she walked into our kitchen, spoiling Paulina with all her favorite dishes. Every afternoon, Paulina gave herself a progesterone injection, prescribed to help the eggs implant. Every morning her grandmother drove her to the clinic to have her hormone levels checked through a blood test. So far, so good. I tried to keep myself distracted with fundraising business on our website.

In the meantime my parents had planned a family trip to a resort in Aspen, Colorado, and offered to pay our way to join them. My sister, Vero, her husband, Juan, and their three kids would be there—Andy could reconnect with his cousins Isabel, Juan Pablo and Dani.

"I'm not travelling," Paulina said. "You and Andy go—as long as we check with Dr. Nurko, and you bring all his medications and formula."

"Are you sure you'll be OK? I hate to miss the pregnancy test."

"Go, go!" She laughed and gave me a little push. "Otherwise you'll be hovering over me, looking for every little symptom and driving me crazy. And I've got Carolina and my *Abuela* with me."

"You'll call me immediately?"

"Go—you're driving me crazy already!"

So in a few days, Andy and I flew to Aspen. I didn't know Paulina was already waking up in the morning nauseated, with sore breasts. She was hiding it from us, afraid to believe what her body was telling her.

On July 10, the day of her pregnancy test, Paulina called me in Colorado. She spoke one word, "Congratulations."

I was so overcome, all I could do was just hand the phone to my mother and then the rest of the family.

PART FOUR

ONE FIT SAVIOR

Chapter Seventeen
Sofía

Paulina's pregnancy went well, after a few initial weeks of bleeding and bed rest—normal after-effects of the fertility treatment hormones. She felt good, and immediately started a pregnancy diary with daily letters to the baby. The entries were mostly trivial—her physical changes and symptoms, as well as details of doctor visits and family activities—but we couldn't wait to include this baby girl in our lives.

Big brother-in-waiting

I recall those nine months as being among the happiest of our married life. Andy, 4, was the happiest of us all. From the moment we told him he would have a baby sister, he was thrilled, excited and impatient. We shared all the ultrasound images with him, so he could watch her grow.

"Mom, can I go inside your stomach and see my sister?"

He helped us shop for a new crib and baby clothes and wanted to share his toys and blankets. I think he believed she'd arrive as a fully equipped play-mate. He loved to measure Paulina's girth with a tape measure, saying, "Mom, my sister grew seven dollars today."

When we chose a name, Sofía, he couldn't wait to tell everyone in his pre-school class. Once the baby started moving, he liked to lie against his mother to feel the kicks. He'd talk to Sofía, tell her stories and kiss his mother's belly.

Andy had a colitis flare up in late summer requiring another hospitalization, but recovered in a few days. Nurko wanted to consider another medication, Remicade, as he continued to try to reduce Andy's steroid dependency. But the immunology team felt it was important to stick to his current regimen.

Every day I told myself, *we just have to keep him safe for another few months.*

Adding to our anxiety was the news that Jordan Orange was leaving Children's Hospital Boston. He and his wife, Katie, decided to move to Philadelphia to be near her family. Jordan had a research position at the University of Pennsylvania and an immunology appointment at Children's Hospital of Philadelphia. They wanted their young daughters, Audrey and Marley, to grow up with their grandparents, aunts, uncles and cousins. Paulina and I understood the desire to be closer to family all too well, but couldn't help feeling abandoned. Dr. Orange had sustained us with medical care and affectionate friendship for two years.

"I wish we could follow him," said Paulina. "I feel like an orphan!"

It was hard to let go, but I knew we'd always include him in ongoing news and updates about Andy.

In October, I found an umbilical cord bank, Viacord, and arranged for their service to collect and store the baby's blood stem cells until Andy was cleared for transplant. When I called, the representative was completely flustered that we were actually planning to *use* the cord blood. For the vast majority of Viacord's customers, umbilical cord banking was simply an insurance policy. The company CEO, Marc D. Beer, got on the line and was very interested in our story. He offered to waive the $1,750 subscription charge, and told me that out of 120,000 customers, only 11 had actually used the stem cells. We'd make it a dozen. When I received the collection kit, I stowed it with Paulina's suitcase, ready to go to the delivery room.

In November, the Make-a-Wish Foundation sent the three of us to Disney World for a week, where both sets of grandparents and Andy's cousins Isabel and Juan Pablo planned to meet us. A black limousine picked us up at our apartment to go to Logan airport and Andy said, "It's just like my toy car, but I'm riding in it!" The Cinderella treatment continued nonstop. In Orlando, we stayed at Give Kids the World, a special hotel serving Make-a-Wish kids and families. When Andy entered the hotel lobby and saw a big wooden castle hung with gilt stars, one of them labeled "Andy," his smile was unlike anything we'd ever seen. With his Make-a-Wish badge, Andy and our entourage bypassed waiting lines and got hugs and autographs from his favorite Disney characters. It was a magical trip to a kingdom of instant gratification. We all needed it.

Pneumonia

The Disney thrill helped Andy get through a difficult Christmas season, when he was hospitalized with pneumonia. Despite all our precautions—limiting social exposure, scrubbing the house with disinfectant, washing our hands until they cracked and bled—he still fell prey to infections most of us could easily fight. Paulina was upset to have to stay home, but we couldn't risk her health too, so I spent the days and nights on the ward with Andy. This hospitalization had its consolations, though. Construction on Children's new clinical building had just begun and from our window Andy and I could watch the workers walking on the high steel beams. "How do they do that?" Andy asked. "Can they fly if they fall?"

"Would you like to send them a message?" I asked. He nodded without taking his eyes from the soaring beams.

I painted a large sign on some cardboard and taped it to the window: "Hi, my name is Andy. You are my heroes."

A few hours later, as we watched, one of the construction workers spray-painted ANDY on a beam and waved to us. By evening there were eight steel beams proclaiming "Andy" in yellow and white letters. He insisted we sleep with the shades open. "That's my name on my building," he told his doctors and nurses.

By late February, we could see Sofía clearly in a three-D ultrasound image. She had big eyes and a round face and was sucking her thumb. All we wanted was to reach out and hold her.

The sweetest sound

The New England Flower Show is a beloved local ritual, a week in late winter when Bostonians are feeling they can't possibly make it until spring. On March 14, 2004, we were strolling through the lush exhibits that transformed the hangar-like Bayside Exposition Center in South Boston. Outside, the day was gray and raw, snow flurries adding to piles of dirty ice. But inside was a garden-lover's fantasy, full of nodding yellow tulips, bubbling fountains and banks of fragrant pink roses. All four of Andy's grandparents were visiting, and he dashed from one display to the next, calling *"¡Mira, mira!* Look!" Paulina and I followed more slowly, hand-in-hand, her partially-buttoned black coat stretched tight across her middle. She'd been having mild contractions and cramps for a week. Suddenly she stopped, pressing a hand to her hard belly.

"I think I want to sit down for a while. Here's a bench—you go ahead." Then, "Actually, I think I want to head to the hospital." She laughed. "Our little girl wants to come out and smell the flowers. We should name her Rosa!"

We sent our parents in their rental car back to the apartment with Andy, and I checked the back of my Jeep where Paulina's overnight bag and the kit from the umbilical cord blood bank had been safely packed for weeks. It was snowing more heavily, and I tried to stay calm as I drove Paulina to Brigham & Women's Hospital, next door to Children's in the Longwood Medical Area. It felt amazing to approach that familiar campus with happy excitement instead of fear and dread. Paulina, who was already bracing herself with hard contractions, said breathlessly,

"This one's moving fast! She doesn't want to wait!"

In less than an hour we were in the delivery room.

"I'm ready to push!" said Paulina.

"You're in a hurry, little Sofía," said the obstetrician, guiding the baby's head as it began to crown. At 6:13 p.m. our daughter entered the world, loudly. Sofía was chubby and perfect, with large dark eyes and bright pink cheeks. *"¡Está lindísima!"* I told Paulina. The most beautiful baby I'd ever seen.

"Listen to that cry! It's the sweetest sound…" Paulina held out her arms.

I watched as the doctor extracted every ounce of blood possible from the umbilical cord, and readied it for shipping to Viacord. "We got 900 units, more than one bag!" she said.

Then I got to hold the swaddled baby.

"Bienvenida, Sofía," I said softly, my voice breaking. "We've been waiting and longing for you."

The next morning, Andy raced into his mother's hospital room ahead of his grandparents. *"¡Mi hermanita linda!* My pretty little sister!" He pulled aside her blankets, stroked her head, kissed her and carefully held her on his lap. He wanted to help change her diaper. He'd even brought along some of his favorite toys. "Do you want to play swords?" he asked Sofía. He was only mildly disappointed to realize she could manage just five activities: eating, sleeping, pooping, peeing and crying. He was fascinated by all of it.

The previous day's snowstorm left the city blanketed. "Boston dressed in white to receive Sofía," I said as we drove home with our new baby, ready to start being a family of four.

Another baptism

Two months later, Andy turned 5 on the same day Sofía was baptized, May 15. We flew to Mexico City for the dual celebration, despite the anxiety and exhaustion of taking all necessary precautions. Andy could bathe only in bottled water, could eat only formula and was restricted to seeing a few people at a time, but it was worth it. We hadn't been home in three years. Andy received so much loving attention he sometimes got overwhelmed. He'd run to me to be picked up, and he'd hide his head in my shoulder for a moment. But he got to play with his cousins and a few other kids, chattering in Spanish all the time, and that made him happier than anything.

The baptism brought hundreds of family members together from both sides—a rare event. My parents asked a close family friend to perform the ceremony. *Padre* Toño was the same priest who had told us that, despite the Church's stance against IVF, in his view our search for Sofía was "the lesser of two evils." Part of our story was coming full circle, and my heart swelled to see Sofía looking like a rosy little cherub in her long white dress. All she needed was a halo.

Afterwards, there was a huge party at my brother Victor's house where our beloved Dr. Roberto Kretschmer showed up. He looked older, grayer and more tired, but still had his booming voice. He greeted Andy just as he had all those nights in the hospital: "How's my little man?" Then he knelt down, stiffly, and opened his arms. Andy stepped right into them.

A few months later, Dr. Kretschmer died of a heart attack. My parents sent me the lengthy newspaper obituary, listing his professional accomplishments and medical contributions. It mentioned his large family and his passion for opera. Paulina and I mourned him on our own. We remembered his tireless search for Andy's diagnosis, his willingness to answer every question, his kindness during every hospitalization. He'd been our lifeline during some of our darkest days. I wished he could have lived long enough to follow our story.

Andrés, Paulina and Andy after an ultrasound at the fertility clinic

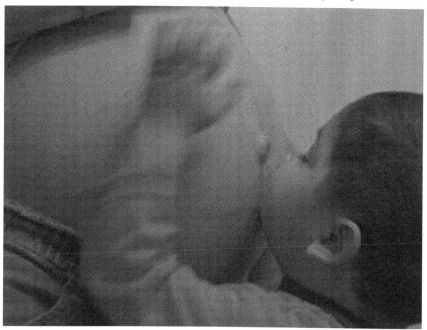

Andy kissing Paulina's belly, at home in Auburndale, MA.

New construction at Children's Hospital Boston.

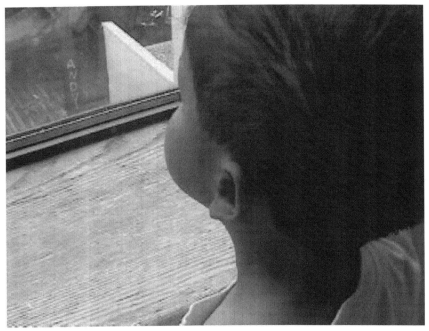

Andy looking out the window at "his" building.

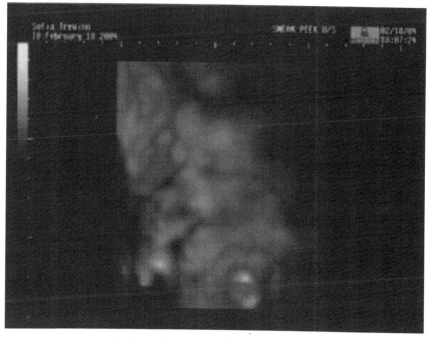

Sofia sucking her thumb in a 3-D ultrasound.

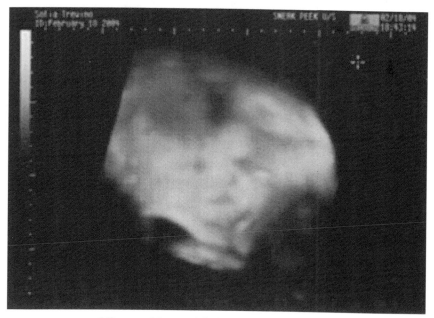

Ultrasound image of Sofia's face, with eyes wide open.

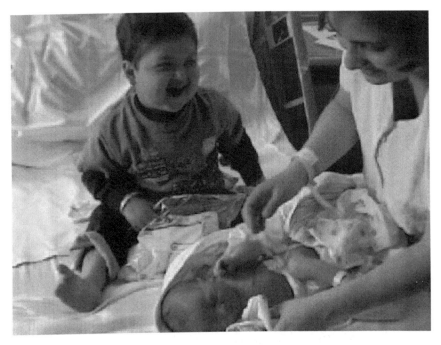

Andy greeting Sofía at Brigham & Women's Hospital.

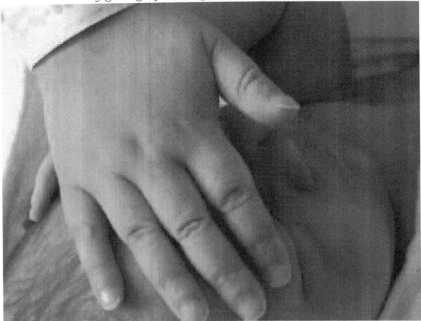

One-day-old Sofía getting ready to go home.

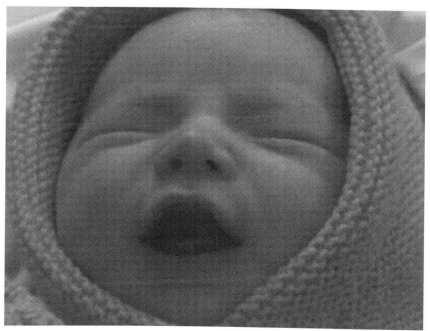

One-day-old Sofía

Big brother, little sister.

Chapter Eighteen
Transplant Prep

In June, Paulina and I met again with Dr. Pai, the transplant specialist. We'd been in touch during Paulina's pregnancy and shared the news of Sofía's birth. Now it was time to proceed with the plan. The encounter was as painful as it had been 16 months ago. Dr. Pai faced us across a large desk. As I suspected she'd been trained to do, she gave us the cold, hard facts.

Her first piece of bad news was that she checked the report from Viacord about the volume of Sofía's collected umbilical cord blood, and it wasn't enough. Andy needed more blood stem cells to supplement the cord blood. They'd have to be taken from his sister's bone marrow.

"But Viacord told us we'd harvested an above-average amount!" I protested. "Why isn't that enough? We don't want the Sofía to go through any kind of medical procedure!"

"Well, it's not enough, and supplemental bone marrow will give your son the best possible chance for a successful transplant. If we wait until Sofía is 6 months old, and has had some of her immunizations, we can be even surer her immune system is healthy and able to cure Andy. Bone marrow harvesting won't harm the baby. It's a safe, relatively painless procedure."

I wasn't convinced. Then the news got worse. Dr. Pai told us she wouldn't use the "mini transplant," with a lighter dose of chemotherapy. We'd hoped for the mini dose ever since Dr. Horwitz, the transplant specialist at the NIH, had suggested it. But Dr. Pai felt there wasn't enough supporting data on Andy's type of disease to risk using it. So he'd be in for the full toxic barrage to completely destroy his bone marrow, his blood-making ability and what was left of his immune system. He might not survive this assault, she stated.

With brutal honesty, she ticked off the list of other risks. The infusion of his sister's blood stem cells might not engraft to Andy's diminished bone marrow. He might develop graft-versus-host disease, where his transplanted cells rejected his body, even though they were from a matched donor. And while the transplant could vanquish the NEMO condition, it might have little effect on his chronic colitis. There were no guarantees. We'd heard all this before, but it was still terrifying. Paulina was on the verge of tears.

I tried to keep my voice steady. "It's taken us so long to have Andy relatively stable on all these medications, even though he has these adrenal crises. Which is better, to practically kill him with chemo and hope the new cells bring him back? Or offer him the best life possible on medication for as long as we can?" I asked.

Dr. Pai lowered her eyes to her desk, and then looked straight at me. "I can only recommend that you proceed with the transplant. It offers the best chance for your son's life," she answered. "I want to do a few more tests on your daughter's compatibility, but I think we could be ready to go ahead in September, after Sofía's had her vaccines."

On the way home, I said to a sobbing Paulina, "Look, it's Dr. Pai's job to tell us about every downside, every risk, every possible side effect. She has to. It doesn't mean Andy's response will necessarily be that way. Let's get another opinion."

A few days later, Dr. Raif Geha, chief of Immunology, welcomed us into his office in Children's new research building. I liked and trusted him. He carried himself with authority, but his dark eyes were warm. He was from Lebanon, and spoke Spanish because his wife was South American. He'd been consulting on Andy's immunology treatment since Dr. Orange left.

Geha was blunt. "Andy's got a double-whammy—his immune deficiency not only makes him prey to all kinds of infections, but it has led to a severely damaged digestive system. As for his meds—the prednisone may be helping his gut, but steroids and immune deficiencies don't do well together. I recently lost three immune-deficient patients who were on cortisones and couldn't find a bone marrow transplant. Andy's unlikely to reach adulthood on his current regimen. If he were my son, I wouldn't hesitate to do the transplant."

He added, "If you believe in any kind of God, now is the time to start praying."

So, we prayed.

In July, Dr. Pai met with us again to go over the 20-page consent form from the Children's/Dana-Farber transplant program. It listed Andy's check-in date as September 13. Later, I sat down at my desk and reviewed its contents while Paulina nursed the baby in the next room. Andy would have to pass a complete physical exam to ensure he was strong enough for the ordeal. He'd need a double lumen central line placed in his heart—two ports to handle all the blood draws, the IV nutrition, the chemo and other meds. He'd be isolated in a protective environment on 6 West, Children's transplant floor. No visitors, no trips outside the room. The "conditioning treatment," the intensive procedure to kill his immune system, would start with four days of an intravenous drug called busulfan, followed by a day of rest, then four days of cyclophosphamide. It was the same regimen Dr. Jain had used for the only other NEMO transplant we knew about. Then, in this totally weakened state, Andy would receive the transfusion of Sofía's cells from her cord blood and her bone marrow. It usually took two-to-four weeks to see a rise in the blood cell count, indicating the new cells had grafted onto Andy's depleted bone marrow and were multiplying. During this time, the effects of the chemo would hit hard. His hair would fall out, his skin would darken, and he'd develop painful ulcers in his mouth and esophagus. Then we'd have another one-to- four weeks of isolation after engraftment before we could go home. The document's final sentence, "Depending on the patient's complications, the entire process can be as short as four weeks or as long as several months," sent my anxiety level soaring all over again.

I will be beside you, Andy, every minute, every day, as long as it takes, I thought.

There was an additional consent form for Sofía's bone marrow donation. The procedure seemed straightforward. Under general anesthesia, she'd get a needle puncture deep into each hip bone, drawing out just enough marrow to supplement the cord blood she'd already given. But I couldn't stop thinking about the possible risks to our baby. *How safe is this? How much bone marrow will be taken? Who is going to perform the procedure? Would there be a chance of any side effects?* I knew I had to get Dr. Pai to answer these questions before I could sign off. To calm myself I wrote her name on a sheet of paper, SOFÍA TRE-VINO, and started playing with the 12 letters.

> SEA OF IN VITRO
>
> I VITAE FOR SON
>
> SO NAÏVE FOR IT
>
> Then, ONE FIT SAVIOR

That's it! I walked into the living room where Paulina was feeding Sofía on the couch in front of the TV, with Andy in his usual spot, nestled close beside them. I showed her my anagram for Sofía's name.

"Well, she is!" she said, kissing the baby's head. "She's truly our savior!"

Hurry up and wait

On the last day of August, Andy had his pre-transplant checkup at Children's. The doctors looked at his heart, liver and gut. They took an intestinal culture in case any infection culprits were lurking, like his nemesis, *citomegalovirus.* Andy wanted to know about every machine and device he encountered.

"Mama, what's that for?" he asked when an ultrasound evaluated his chest veins for the central line he'd get in a few weeks. He'd forgotten all about central lines. I knew we were going to have to explain his transplant to him, and I had no idea how.

Then we got a tour of 6 West, the stem cell transplant unit. It consisted of 13 private rooms, a kitchen and family room, parent bathrooms, playroom, nurses' stations, doctor's office and meeting room. We entered the unit through an airlock, and the whole floor had sterile, filtered air. The patient rooms included bathrooms labeled *For Patient Use Only,* parent beds, desktop computers with Internet access, a Sony PlayStation, TV and DVD players. There was programmable overhead lighting that could change color. *Good for patients spending a lot of time staring at the ceiling,* I thought.

"Why do you have PlayStations and computers here, but not on the other floors?" I asked the tour nurse.

"Because children suffer more here," she answered quietly.

Andy thought it was a great room. "It's like a hotel, like Disney!"

Paulina started to explain why he'd be staying in a room like this soon, but faltered as soon as Andy looked up at her with his innocent, expectant face. She gave me an agonized look, so I said, "Andy, remember when I told you about the little fish in your stomach, the ones that don't know how to behave? That little fish needs to be replaced with some that swim better and feel OK. And guess what? It turns out Sofía also has those fish in her stomach and she will give you some to replace yours."

"Really?"

"Yes. And your little fish's name is NEMO."

He laughed; he'd seen the movie *Finding Nemo* many times. "How do they do that, put new fish in me?"

"Well, it's just like when you receive your IV with gamma globulin from

George. The little fish are so small you can't see them but they'll go in through tubes and a pump right into your body. The only difference is that instead of an IV, you'll have a central line here on your chest. You'll get some other medicine too, and it might make you feel a little sick. You and I will stay in the hospital until the new little fish are all settled."

"Will I be able to play with the PlayStation?"

"Of course! And I'll be with you the whole time."

On September 7, we received word that our transplant date was postponed until the 20th. The Transplant Unit on 6 West was completely full with more urgent cancer patients. Andy would have to wait. But the postponement had an up-side. School was starting and Andy got to spend time with his new kindergarten class. Even though he'd be in a special room with restricted contact with other kids, we knew there was some risk involved. But we couldn't deny him something he wanted so much. He came home each afternoon to report to Sofía on everything he'd done.

His greatest happiness continued to be his sister. From the moment we brought her home he was content to spend hours watching her. Sofía was brimming with bright-eyed, red-cheeked energy and hardly napped. She smiled and cooed, grabbed objects and rolled over ahead of schedule. She astounded us with each healthy-baby milestone because Andy's babyhood had been anything but normal.

I decided to make the most of the break, as a family. We went to the movies and the mall. We went swimming in the local hotel pool. We played lots of music at home and jumped and danced around. Every night before his bath we let Andy run naked through the apartment, laughing and calling, "Catch me!"

One evening I asked, "Andy, what would you like to do tomorrow?"

"I want to ride in a helicopter!"

I knew it was extravagant, but I had to grant his wish. While Paulina and the baby stayed home, Andy and I drove to New York for the day and took a helicopter ride above Manhattan. He looked absurdly tiny strapped into his seat, wearing an enormous pair of headphones, but as we circled the Statue of Liberty he was so happy and excited I couldn't get enough of watching him.

As soon as we landed he said, "Let's go again!"

But we had to head home and get ready for the transplant. Andy helped pack his own suitcase, saying importantly, "Dr. Pai invited me to spend the night at the hospital."

At my insistence, Paulina had reluctantly agreed that I would stay around-the-clock with Andy throughout this ordeal. The baby was still breastfeeding and needed her mother. Paulina would visit whenever she could, thanks to a wonderful babysitter she found through our church—a Guatemalan woman named Claudia whose accent reminded us of folks in Chiapas. Still, it was a 45-minute trip from Auburndale to Children's and the thought of the distance and separation made Paulina so tense and tearful I got irritated. I wanted to soothe her but I was having a hard time managing my own anxiety. The more I distanced myself, the sadder and more withdrawn Paulina became, and I knew she felt emotionally abandoned.   I just couldn't focus on anything but Andy. Implicitly, we understood we'd each chosen to deal with our pain and sadness separately. After what we'd survived so far, I wanted to believe we respected and trusted each other enough to know we were still a tight team. I'd been relieved when Lupita arrived the previous week, laden with special gifts for Andy to pack for the hospital. I knew that at least for a while Paulina would get the kind of support she needed from her mother.

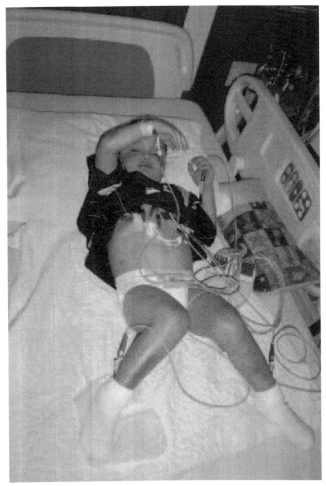

Andy during an echocardiogram, on 6 West.

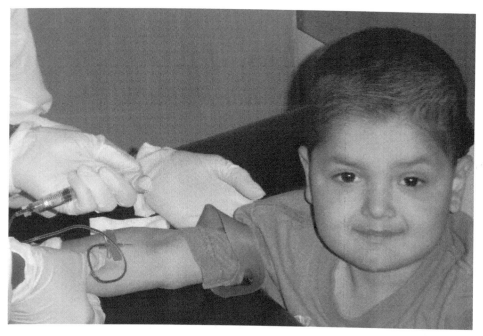

Andy having blood drawn.

Andy and the helicopter ride, New York.

Andy at home, packing for his transplant.

Chapter Nineteen
6 West

We checked into 6 West on September 20. Andy got a painless regular IV line from his friend George, the burly Irish nurse who was a genius at finding veins. I said, as I always did, "George, one day I'll erect a statue in your honor, with a plaque that says, *it didn't hurt a bit.*"

And he answered, as he always did, "Thanks, but I'd rather have a house on an island."

"Are they going to plug me into a bottle?" Andy asked him.

"Yes, I think later you're going to get Sofía's stem cells," George told him matter-of-factly.

With an IV dose of anesthesia, Andy went into the OR for his central line placement. When he came out he had a new double lumen catheter in his chest, with one white-capped line for chemo and medication infusion, and a red-capped one for blood draws. It looked very familiar, just like old times.

"I have my central line?" he asked as the anesthesia wore off. His voice was ragged.

"Yes, my champion, you did very well. You have your central line," answered Paulina, kissing him. I could tell it was a struggle for her, seeing him once again attached to tubes.

He noticed he was connected to a heart monitor and could make the green line on the screen move up when he held his breath. He grinned. "Papa, look what I'm doing!" he whispered.

"That means your vital signs are improving, young man," said the recovery room nurse as she disconnected the cables. We transported his bed up the elevator to the 6th floor, then through the air-lock entrance of 6 West.

Paulina kissed us goodbye. She had to go home to feed the baby. Andy and I unpacked our bags and I set up my laptop, my essential connection to the outside world. Then we inspected the room together. The window faced "his" new building, still under construction. We checked out every pump, air vent and call button and counted 42 electrical outlets. Andy tried out a game on the room's personal computer and checked all the channels on the TV. We had a direct phone line and we called home to say "hi" to Mom and Sofía.

At 6:00 the next morning, a pretty young woman entered the room introduced herself, "Hello, Mr. Andy, my name is Kelli and I'll be your primary nurse while you're here." He nodded shyly, suddenly speechless.

"Did you hear there's a monkey on the floor?" she asked. No comment from Andy.

Then we heard, "UH UH AH AH EH EHEH!"

Andy jumped off his bed and looked around.

"Did you hear that? That's the monkey," said Kelli calmly as she took Andy's pulse. Her mouth had barely moved.

"UH UHUH AH AH EH EHEHEH!" We heard it again. Andy started laughing.

"Andy, someone told me there's a dolphin here also—have you seen him?" asked Kelli. "TRIIT TRIIT CRUITT CRUITT TRIIT!" she called, standing on her tiptoes and waved her arms.

Andy jumped up and down on his bed, asking for more. "A dolphin, a dolphin!" He didn't want Kelli to leave the room. She hooked up a tube to his central line and gave him his first chemo infusion. The pump was labeled:

Cytotoxic Chemical. Caution: Special Handling Precautions.

That afternoon he got his second chemo dose. "When will he lose his hair?" I asked Kelli.

"In a week or two. Don't worry, he'll do fine."

Setback

The next day, I waited for the 6 a.m. chemo. It didn't come. Then a doctor I didn't recognize entered the room. "I have some bad news and good news," he said. "We just discovered last night Andy's *cytomegalovirus* culture came back positive. We have to stop the chemo and delay the transplant. The risk of developing a severe infection is very high."

My heart plummeted. Our old enemy, always hiding in Andy's intestines, needed no invitation to multiply.

"But the good news is we caught the *cytomegalovirus* infection early and can start treating it immediately. We'll give him a five-day antiviral treatment, and take another culture. Then we can start the chemo all over again."

"Will it harm him, having the extra chemo?"

"He should be fine, but we'll keep a close eye on him."

I called Paulina. More tears. She wanted to be in the hospital with us, but had to stay with Sofía until Claudia, the babysitter, could come the following day. I posted the news on our website, and received a note from Jordan Orange in Philadelphia:

"OLD ENEMIES DIE HARD. HANG IN THERE."

We were hanging all right.

That afternoon Andy was nauseated. The transplant unit didn't have his Neocate formula so we'd urged him to eat regular food for lunch, which was still very difficult for him. He vomited and Kelli gave him some anti-nausea medication. That night he was restless, occasionally gagging without waking up, talking in his sleep, "I want a ball," and "Get behind me! I told you that I want... Mama! Papa!"

When I told his night nurse she said, "Maybe the nausea medicine is making him a bit loopy."

In the morning, Andy woke and tried to drink some milk, but he was pale and dizzy and dropped the cup. The nurse of the day, a smiling young woman named Maura, came in and greeted him sweetly. She placed her stethoscope against his chest, and her face turned serious.

"His heart rate is too fast." She connected Andy to a monitor—*pulse 205,* it read. While I held him, Maura tried a blood pressure cuff, but couldn't get a reading. "I'll be right back—I'm getting the doctor," she said, running from the room. Andy drooped against me, his eyes blank.

"Andy? Are you OK? Andy!" *It must be those two chemo doses, it's poisoning him!* I started praying. *Please, we're so close. This can't be happening!*

Several doctors rushed into the room, surrounding his bed. Glancing at

Andy's chart, one quickly introduced herself, "I'm Leslie Lehmann, the attending physician." She turned to Maura, the nurse. "So he has a *CMV* infection?" Two other nurses entered, pushing a gray cart loaded with instruments and medication vials.

Maura answered, "I'm losing his vital signs, he seems to be going into shock!"

Suddenly, I realized what was happening. "It's not the *cytomegalovirus*, it's adrenal failure!" I told them. "He has adrenal dysfunction, he's in shock, and he needs stress steroids!"

The team mobilized instantly. Dr. Lehmann said, "OK, let's get the steroids." The charge nurse answered, "Here's the syringe, right into the central line now…here we go…"

Dr. Lehmann watched as Andy's pulse normalized and his blood pressure returned. She stroked his head, saying, "That's good, that's the way." After a few minutes Andy spoke in a weak voice.

"Papá, me vomité en mi camiseta…I threw up on my shirt…"

"¿Te sientes mejor? Do you feel better now?" I asked, holding him. He nodded.

Dr. Lehmann smiled at me and then left. Nurse Maura stayed with us all afternoon and evening, keeping watch on Andy's monitors. Andy was asleep when Paulina arrived later. I started crying as soon as I told her, "It was the same story. He was in shock, his vitals signs dropped—he was almost gone."

We hadn't even started the transplant treatment and already we'd experienced one of our worst nightmares.

Persistent foes

Andy slept soundly that night, waking only when the pump infusing fluids into his central line began beeping. Before the nurse came in to fix it, he muttered,

"Ay esta pinche bomba. This damn pump."

In the morning, he told me, "Dad, I really am feeling better." I was grateful. He needed to muster all his strength for what lay ahead.

I worked hard to keep Andy entertained while we waited for the antivirals to work. We played with Andy's action figures and watched videos. Paulina visited almost every day with reports about Sofía, which Andy loved. "¿Está comiendo cereal? She's eating cereal?" he'd say. "¿Puré de manzana? Apple sauce?" He had such difficulty with any food other than his formula he was astounded at what his sister would put in her mouth.

On the sixth day, Jordan Orange surprised us with a visit. He'd come up from Philadelphia for a weekend conference. There was no one I was happier to see. He brought Andy a gift—a beautiful snow globe with a miniature Boston inside. He shook it to show Andy the mesmerizing swirl of flakes.

"Is Children's Hospital inside?" Andy asked, squinting at the tiny city in the snow.

Jordan said, "Maybe you can see it if you look hard. Remember, Andy, when the snow arrives outside your window, you'll be feeling better."

"We'll be watching, won't we, Andy?" I said. Jordan and I ate lunch together in the hospital cafeteria, and he reaffirmed for me that going ahead with the transplant was the right decision. I wished with all my heart we could have Jordan Orange beside us for the next step of our ordeal.

Nurse Kelli came back after a few days off, and Andy couldn't wait for the monkey and dolphin sounds. "Have you ever seen The Worm?" she asked him.

"The Worm?" He shook his head.

Kelli moved a chair, stretched out her arms, then threw herself stomach-down on the floor. With her arms and legs extended, she arched and curled in a series of sinuous inch-worm moves. We watched in disbelief. Then she hopped up to her feet, dusted off her hands. "That was The Worm," she said.

We applauded, and then Andy fell laughing on his bed, holding his central line carefully. He arched his back and wiggled, "The Worm!"

After five days, we got the latest *cytomegalovirus* culture result. It was still positive—Andy needed the antivirals for two more weeks.

I tried to be upbeat. "Well, at least every doctor and nurse on 6 West is getting to know Andy really well. That can only help," I said to Paulina.

The hours and days dragged on, and even PlayStation lost its charm. Andy had become an avid baseball fan, and the Boston Red Sox provided a welcome distraction as the play-offs proceeded to the World Series. Miraculously, the Sox won the championship for the first time in 86 years. It was a hysterical, historic moment all over the city. Even 6 West buzzed in celebration.

But Andy kept begging to go home. On our 19th day in the unit, Dr. Pai allowed us to leave the hospital for a few hours. Andy was taking so many antivirals and antibiotics we figured it would be safe. It was a beautiful, mild October day and we met up with Paulina and Sofía in a park on the Charles River near our apartment. Andy was ecstatic, hugging and kissing his little sister. Sofía was healthy and happy, bouncing in my arms. She'd had her 6-month vaccinations. She was pushing herself up to sit. Her laugh was irresistible. Andy noticed the vivid trees, the wind ruffling the river, the brilliant blue sky, and pointed them all out to Sofía. Too soon, the afternoon ended and we returned to 6 West.

Trouble continues

The third *cytomegalovirus* culture came back positive. We started another antiviral round, this time a stronger dosage that kept Andy tethered to an infusion pump 24 hours a day. He was very careful of his central line, even in his sleep he never let the tubes get tangled. He now pushed the nurse call button himself when his pump started beeping. He'd mastered the hospital routine and submitted without complaint: vital signs checked every four hours, day and night; blood sample before 4:00 a.m.; weight checked at 8 a.m.; prayers with a chaplain at 9 a.m.; in bed ready for mid-morning doctor rounds; a bath in the afternoon where we checked his central line for any problems. I always changed his sheets before evening, and mopped the floor with disinfectant. Andy was also on contact precautions again—nurses and doctors entered in masks and gowns. Even his mother had to decontaminate for every visit, scrubbing with antibacterial soap.

Paulina was having increasing difficulty being away from Andy. She called many times a day, starting with an early morning request for Andy's vital signs. I was posting regular, detailed updates in a blog on the www.andy.org.mx website, but she always wanted more.

"When I'm at home with Sofía, I feel like I need to be with Andy, and when I'm here I feel like I should be with Sofía," she complained on her next visit. "I'm just bouncing between two places. It's exhausting. We've always cared for him together, but now when I come to the hospital, I feel like a stranger. Some of the nurses don't even acknowledge me."

I was getting impatient. "Well, it's hard on both of us. I don't like being separated from you and Sofía, either, but that's just the way it has to be for now."

Her voice rose. "I feel like you're taking ownership of Andy's situation and shutting me out. I can't stand it that you're not sharing every bit of information with me. You're ignoring me!" she accused. "And you're flirting with the nurses!"

Now I was angry. "That's crazy! I'm not taking control, and I'm definitely not flirting just because I talk to the nurses! I'm simply trying to make this as good an experience as possible for Andy. We're in this together: you take care of Sofía because she needs you, and I'm taking care of Andy because you can't be here!" Then, "Look, we're both tired. But we're almost there. We just need to get rid of the *cytomegalovirus*, and then move ahead. Sofía needs to be healthy for the bone marrow donation, and you're doing a great job taking care of her."

Paulina started to cry. "What's happening to *us*, to our relationship? When will we ever have time for ourselves, together, just you and me? Why can't we leave Andy with his nurse for just a few hours and do something together, go to a café, take a walk? You can't focus on me for a minute, you're so obsessed with Andy."

I hugged her briefly, but I just didn't have the energy to comfort her more. "We haven't had time for us in five years. But that's why we're here; we're going to fix the situation for Andy, and for ourselves. Soon we'll have time together." It wasn't enough, but it was all I could give.

Dr. Pai visited a few nights later and I asked her, "What if *cytomegalovirus* returns after the transplant, when we're waiting for the new cells to take hold? How soon would Sofía's cells help him fight it off?"

I could hear Kretschmer's voice in my head, "Absence of proof is not a proof of absence."

"It would take at least 100 days for the transplanted cells to be able to take care of a *cytomegalovirus* infection," Dr. Pai answered. "In the meantime, we'd have to rely on the antivirals and gamma globulin to keep him safe." She paused, and with uncharacteristic sympathy in her voice, she said, "You can still choose not to do with the transplant, you know."

"No. We're going ahead."

Andy on a few hours' leave from Children's Hospital.

Sofía and Andy playing at home in Auburndale, MA.

Sofía and Andrés at home in Auburndale, MA.

Chapter Twenty
The Go-Ahead

On October 19, after a full month on 6 West, the *cytomegalovirus* culture came back negative at last. On Andy's website, I announced we were starting the chemo tomorrow, and asked for prayers that the *cytomegalovirus* would remain inactive. Andy's 10-day contact precaution was lifted so he could go out into the corridor. It gave us a breath of fresh air—literally purified by the unit's high-tech ventilation system. Andy loved greeting the other transplant kids through their hallway windows, clowning to make them laugh, especially the babies. He missed Sofía.

"Tomorrow's an important day. You're going to start chemo again," I told him. "Are we ready?" After so many days together, we communicated almost without speaking.

He nodded, watching somberly as I scrubbed the floors, used alcohol wipes on his toys, and even cleaned the walls and windows. I'd explained to him that his defenses would be low, and we didn't want any germs lingering.

The first chemo infusion, the busulfan, started at 6 a.m. October 20. Within days, his daily blood level chart showed his blood cells were dying, as his absolute neutrophil count, or ANC, started dropping from its high of 2,220. In nine days, it would be around zero. He'd have no disease resistance at all. He'd be ready for the transplant.

The last days of chemo, on the second chemo drug, cyclophosphamide, were difficult. Andy stopped being interested in play, he wanted only to sleep.

Paulina commented, "It's like watching his battery run down and his lights dim."

We were both bracing ourselves not just for the transplant, but also for Sofía's bone marrow donation. Despite Dr. Pai's reassurances, I imagined all the things that might go wrong. I wondered if we would ever have gone through the baby-making ordeal if we'd known Sofía's donation would be more than just her umbilical blood.

By October 28, the day before the transplant, nausea had destroyed his appetite, and he was relying on intravenous nutrition. That evening, his nurse Kelli came in to give him anti-nausea medication. It was almost Halloween and she was wearing a green cap sprouting a wig, a pair of antennae and two round, googly eyes.

"This hat will scare away your nausea, Andy," she said. Andy laughed for the first time in days. Kelli medicine was good medicine.

Paulina called to say that she and Sofía would be in early the next morning, and Sofía's bone marrow aspiration was scheduled for 8 a.m. Then her stem-cell rich marrow blood and the stored cord blood would be ready for the transfusion. Paulina also mentioned that Sofía had started crawling that day. She was just 7 months old.

Before I went to sleep, I wrote to Sofía on our website:

Sofía, tomorrow you will share the most valuable gift in the entire world—a chance for life itself.

You are made of "the right stuff." We can only hope and pray to God that Andy is able to make good use of these cells and win the battle against NEMO.

Remember your brother is even bigger than his body, and only God knows the outcome of this battle.

I believe from the bottom of my heart and even from my bone marrow that Andy will win. He will keep on sharing with us that wonderful smile and in a few months he will be able to say to you, "THANK YOU!"

Transplantation day

"Sofía!" Andy shouted, sitting up in bed, holding out his arms. It was October 29, 2004—the big day. We'd gotten permission for Sofía to briefly visit the floor before her procedure. Halloween was only two days away, and Paulina had dressed her in costume. Sofía was the cutest ladybug Andy and I had ever seen. Andy longed to touch her, but also understood that he couldn't. His ANC count was close to zero; his immune system was gone. I could see the effort he made, holding back his hugs and kisses. He wanted his sister to demonstrate her new trick, and she obliged, crawling smartly down the corridor while he watched from his window.

My parents and Paulina's had flown in from Mexico, and we felt buoyed by their support. When it was time for the bone marrow harvest, Paulina was fine with my being the one to accompany Sofía to the OR for the anesthesia. Our friend George had inserted an IV in Sofía's hand, so gently she didn't even notice. It was there in case she needed a blood transfusion.

I dressed in a blue gown, hat and facemask, which Sofía kept pulling at. The anesthesiologist had explained earlier they'd use gas to put her under.

"Dad, you may choose the flavor of the gas mask for her—bubble gum or cherry?" the nurse asked.

"Let's do bubble gum."

"As soon as she breathes through this mask, she won't feel or remember a thing."

I kissed my daughter, *"Adios, Sofía. Te quiero mucho.* 'Bye, Sofía. I love you very much."

She fell asleep on the first breath.

Please God, take care of her, I prayed.

The procedure took less than 90 minutes. Paulina joined me, and when they called us into the recovery room, Sofía was sitting up in her crib, eating a red popsicle. She smiled at us.

"She did great!" said the nurse. "She didn't need a transfusion afterwards." Sofía had a Band-Aid on each thigh, covering two barely visible needle pricks. She waved a musical toy playing, "If you're happy and you know it clap your hands," and she bounced happily to the tune.

Fingers crossed

As soon as Sofía was out of the recovery room, she and Paulina were assigned a room on the 7th floor. Paulina's mother joined them there, and I returned to 6 West.

"Andy, tu hermana fué muy valiente." Your sister was very brave," I told him. "She was dancing in her crib."

He smiled. *"¿Donde está ahorita?* Where is she now?"

"She's up on the 7th floor with Mom. Her little fish will be here shortly."

He wanted to walk a bit in the corridor, so we did, with my mother pushing his infusion pump. On the way back, we saw two small plastic bags, full of bright red blood, sitting at the nurses' station. One contained Sofía's cord blood, the other, her bone marrow.

We helped Andy back into bed. His nurse Michelle Lanni entered with the first red bag attached to a tube, and hung it on his infusion pump. I was playing music softly on my computer—Bach's *Unaccompanied 'Cello Suites*. No one said a word as the nurse connected the tube to his central line, unclamped it, and the infusion began. The first bag emptied, and Michelle connected the second bag.

My parents stood at the foot of the bed, holding their clasped hands against their chests. They didn't take their eyes off Andy.

He lay on his back, arms at his side, face serious, eyes closed. Then I saw his left hand. He had crossed his fingers.

I signaled to my parents and they followed my eyes to his crossed fingers. They both raised their hands to their faces, and I saw the tears seeping through.

I took a deep breath, swallowed hard. "You relax, Andy. Everything will go well."

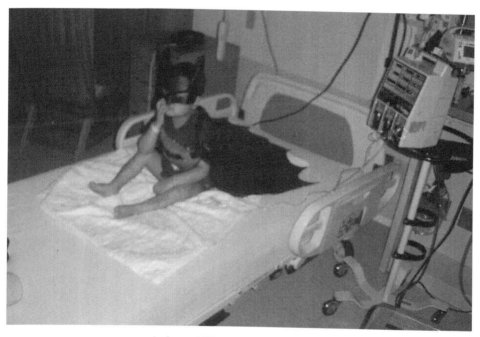

Andy on 6 West, waiting for transplant day.

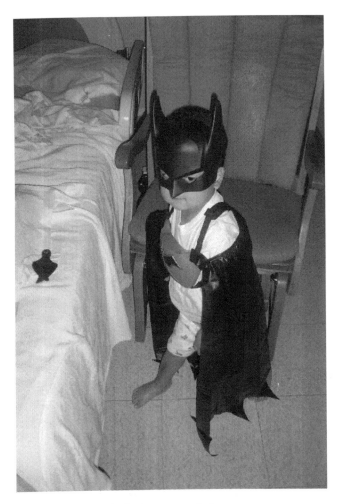

Andy during cytomegalovirus treatment.

First dose of chemo on 6 West.

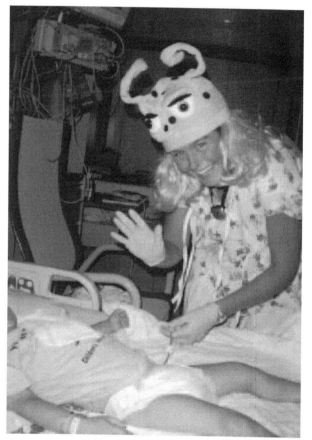

Nurse Kelli with Andy on 6 West.

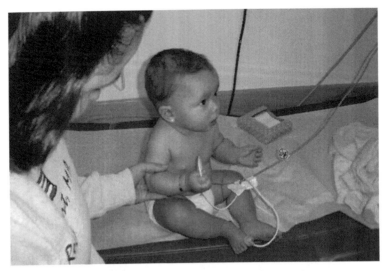

Paulina with Sofía, preparing for bone marrow donation.

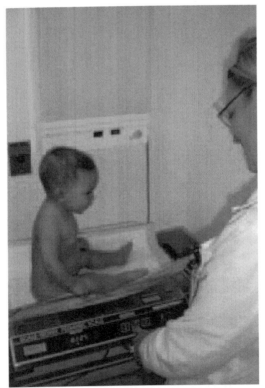

Sofía just prior to bone marrow donation.

The cutest ladybug on Halloween.

Sofía and Andrés before the bone marrow procedure.

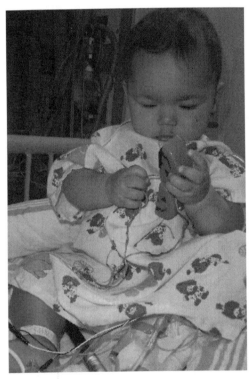

Sofía, minutes after her bone marrow donation.

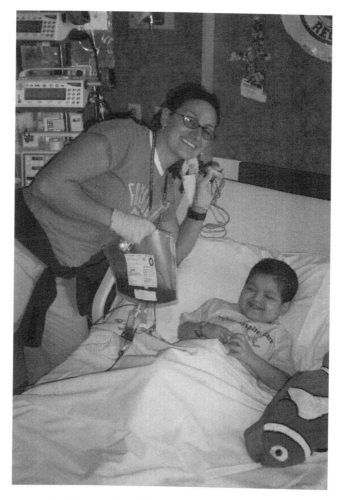

Andy with nurse Michelle Lanni and a bag of Sofia's stem cells.

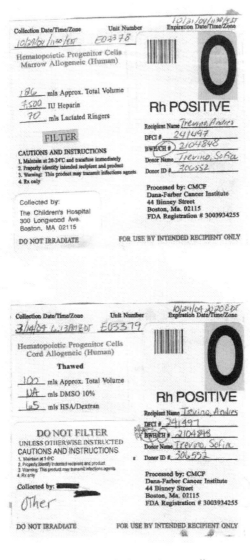

Labels from the bags of stem cells.

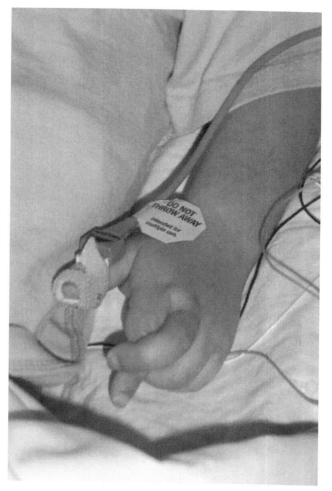

Andy's hand during the stem cell infusion.

Chapter Twenty-One
100 Days

The night of the transplant, the boys bedded down on 6 West, and the girls on 7 East. The nurses had placed a sign on the door of our room:

HAPPY NEW MARROW!

OCTOBER 29, 2004

In the sign's center were the labels from the stem cell infusion bags.

Andy finally slept, but I couldn't. Now we faced the final long, slow climb. It would take 100 days for Andy's new immune system to be functional. It felt like 100 years. I knew I'd have to focus on shorter goals, like the rising absolute neutrophil count. We might begin to see signs of engraftment at 10 to 15 days, showing the new cells had found their way to Andy's marrow and were producing blood cells. White cells first, then red, then other immune cells. I imagined Sofía's cells, and what they would find there.

The new stem cells are arriving at a deserted battleground, a place where years of intense fighting has occurred. A battleground that has seen enemies like listeria monocytogenes, streptococcus bovis, escherichia coli, clostridium difficile, cytomegalovirus, candida albicans and staphylococci. The previous warriors, with their damaged defenses, are dead and gone. They lost many battles because they couldn't produce a protein called nuclear factor kappa B. They had no weapons to fight the enemies. But the new stem cells do. They will become the new warriors, with full defenses. Stem cells, please find your way to Andy's bone marrow. You're needed there. On your way heal the wounds left from other battles. You are welcome, please feel at home.

Day four.

Andy started to lose his hair. He laughed when he woke to find it all over his pillow. He thought it was cool. Paulina very carefully trimmed what was left with snub-nosed scissors. I shaved my head to keep him company. His would grow back, but mine wouldn't—I barely had any left anyway.

Day six.

Andy began to suffer with painful mouth and throat ulcers, a common chemo side effect. Chemo's toxicity damages the cells of mucous membranes, causing an inflammation called mucositis. In Andy's case, the lesions extended throughout his digestive tract. It would clear up as the chemo gradually left his body. Meanwhile, he couldn't eat and had trouble sleeping, waking every half hour to spit out blood and tissue. In addition to anti-inflammatory steroids, he was put on morphine. It came with a manual pain pump Kelli taught him to control himself.

"He can decide for himself when he needs more of the pain medication. I think he's old enough to manage it," she said. "We've found that kids do better at it than parents, who tend to give too much. There's a safeguard on the pump to prevent a serious overdose." It was the first time in his life Andy could make his own treatment decision.

"*El dolor es temporal, se va a ir pronto.* The pain will go away—this is only temporary," I told him. I don't know if he believed me.

Day eight.

His skin darkened and became maddeningly itchy, and he lost his long eyelashes. His mouth was so sore he couldn't open it, even to talk. Paulina brought in a video of Sofía dancing to music–standing up in her crib, wagging her head and shoulders, laughing the whole time. It was the only thing that could coax a smile from Andy.

Day ten.

Andy received a blood boost—a platelet transfusion.

We could see from the window that the trees had lost their leaves and people were walking by in winter coats. I remembered Jordan Orange's promise— *When the snow comes, you'll be feeling better.* I found myself wishing for a blizzard.

Day eleven.

Andy's mouth stopped bleeding, but the sores persisted. He was still using the morphine button, when he wasn't sleeping, which was most of the time. Paulina sat next to his bed for several hours every day, knitting while he napped. The nurses told us the sleeping was typical when new cell production was under way. I wanted to believe it. His ANC count was 110. Were these his own defective cells, left over from the chemo? Or healthy new ones? The ANC had to be above 500 for three consecutive days before the beginning of engraftment was official.

Day twelve.

Andy said, "*Quiero que venga mi hermanita linda…*   "I want my cute little sister to come." We both missed Sofía. Then he told me he was hungry. I ordered a sandwich, carrots, pasta and cookies, and he ate a bite of each.

His ANC was 312. He received another platelet transfusion. That afternoon, Dr. Lehmann, the attending physician, looked at his chart and commented, "I think it's safe to say that we're seeing the new cells in his blood count. After the intense chemo he had, these could only be the new cells."

I immediately called Paulina, "It's the signal we've been waiting for! The new stem cells have reached the bone marrow and the white blood cells are showing up!"

Day thirteen.

Andy's entire digestive tract was still a battleground. His nausea was persistent and his diarrhea constant and painful, sometimes bloody. Dr. Pai was the attending that day and during rounds she said, "The good news is that his ANC today reached 410. He will officially engraft soon, knock on wood. But the bad news is we got a positive *cytomegalovirus* culture again. We'll have to lower his steroids, begin antivirals, and give him an extra dose of antibodies." While still ultra-professional, she had become warmer and more sympathetic during Andy's weeks on 6 West. I sensed she was as disappointed in this news as I was.

Old enemies, I thought. *We've been expecting you. But the new cells will soon put up a fight.*

Paulina took it hard when she arrived that evening. After Andy fell asleep, she said in an agonized whisper, "I feel like we're going backwards again! What if we've only made things worse with the transplant? What if his stomach can't recover from the chemo effects? What if it can't get better?"

I tried to keep my voice down but I was losing my temper, "Stop being negative! We have to believe things *will* get better. It takes time, and we have to focus on the positive. You're undermining the whole process!"

Immediately, I regretted my words, as Paulina's face crumpled in tears. I led her into the only private space on the floor—the roomy parent bathroom in the corridor. We locked the door and held each other. I made amends the best way I knew how. Afterwards we both felt better.

Day fourteen.

Andy's ANC was 820. His army was gaining new recruits. "Way to go, Andy!" I told him. "We're getting there!"

Day sixteen.

A snowstorm had begun as we went to sleep the night before, and by morning we woke to a full blizzard. I carried Andy to the window so he could lift the shade on a white world. He spoke with difficulty, "*¿Papá, donde está el regalo de Dr. Orange?* Where's my present, that Dr. Orange gave me?"

I handed him the snow globe as the nurse came in for his morning blood count. ANC: 1000. He'd been over 500 for three consecutive days. I triumphantly emailed Jordan Orange in Philadelphia: *"You're a magician! You predicted Andy would be feeling better when we saw snow from our window. Well, we're having a blizzard today and Andy's now officially engrafted!"*

The 6 West staff hung a banner outside Andy's room:

HAPPY ENGRAFTMENT DAY! November 14, 2004.

The increasing blood count was a steady beat of positive news every morning. Over the next six weeks, our biggest challenge, as usual, was to vanquish *cytomegalovirus* with antivirals, waiting for the new immune system to be strong enough to fight back. And to repair the damage done by the chemo.

Dr. Pai visited us daily. I liked and trusted her now. She described her job once as being required to drop patients and families off a cliff, then having to run to catch them before they reached the bottom. I understood that part of her job was to be brutally honest.

Gradually, Andy had hours when he felt better. We were both bored, we missed Sofía and we longed to be home. But with the help of our nurses and clinical assistants we had some fun, too. Andy could forget his discomfort for a while playing games on the computer, or dressing up in one of his costumes. When he wasn't on contact precautions, he loved going out of his room into the corridor to show off his Spiderman or Power Rangers outfits.

Another one of our favorite pastimes was a "creepy crawler oven" Paulina brought in one day. We created hundreds of toy bugs using colored plastic goo, molds and a small electric heating oven. The rubbery crawlers it yielded, when hidden in strategic places like a diaper, were great for scaring nurses, at least one time each.

I transformed Andy's room into a tent by hanging half a dozen bed sheets from the ceiling, until one nurse complained we were creating a fire hazard.

Scavenger hunts were popular with our nurse Kelli. We hid clues on post-it notes all around our room.

Our room was located right next to the nurses' station, and nights when Andy couldn't sleep we tapped on the wall until they tapped back. Best of all were the times Kelli was the night nurse and threw a dance party. I'd find the right tunes on my computer, Kelli would bring in conga drums for Andy to play, and she would dance, inviting other nurse to stop by. We got to see more of "The Worm" in action.

Home

By Thanksgiving, Dr. Pai and Dr. Lehmann told Paulina and me that if Andy's latest *cytomegalovirus* culture came back negative, he'd be able to go home in about two weeks. We weren't entirely out of the woods yet, and setbacks like *cytomegalovirus* would undoubtedly occur, but they felt confident enough that Andy could continue healing at home.

Our apartment had to be prepared. The burden of that fell mostly to Paulina. But her mother, Lupita, and two of her aunts, Ana José and Maguis, had been doing relay visits all fall, and they were an enormous gift. They helped move furniture to make the place easier to clean, scrubbed everything down and installed Purell dispensers and boxes of Clorox wipes in every room. We had to keep Andy safe from germs until his new immune system matured.

On December 11, Andy was cleared to go home. He'd have to be isolated for another six months: no visitors, no restaurants, no supermarkets, no friend's house and no school. He'd have to visit the clinic on a daily basis, wearing a facemask, and keep his central line for a while longer. Just in case.

But we couldn't have been happier. Andy gave every nurse and clinical assistant in the transplant unit a big hug. They gave him two hand-decorated T-shirts—one Spider Man, one Finding Nemo, autographed by everyone. We packed up our clothes, computer and toys.

"See you later," Andy said to his friends on 6 West, and we passed through the airlock. We'd been there for 82 days.

Paulina and Sofía were waiting with the car. Sitting next to his sister in the back seat, Andy couldn't stop grinning as we drove home through snowy streets in the waning afternoon. But he was tired when we arrived at our Auburndale apartment. He wanted to relax with Sofía in front of the TV on the carpeted living room floor. He drank some of his formula, laughing at an excited Sofía as Paulina removed the baby's snowsuit and set her down. Instead of plunking on her knees and crawling to him, Sofía stayed standing. Before our astonished eyes, she slowly lurched six steps forward—her very first—until she reached Andy. She crowed triumphantly when he grabbed her hand and raised it as if they were champions crossing a finish line together. Andy was home.

Sign on Andy's room on 6 West.

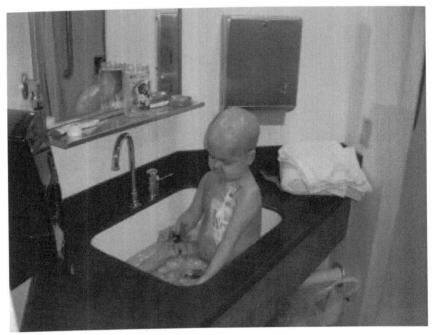

Andy taking a bath on 6 West.

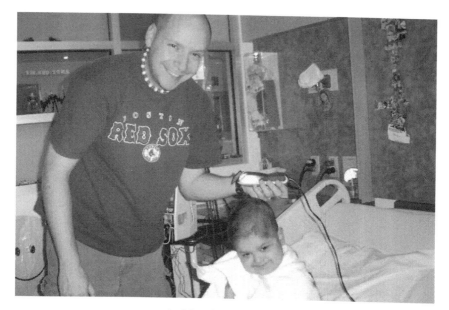

Andrés trimming Andy's hair.

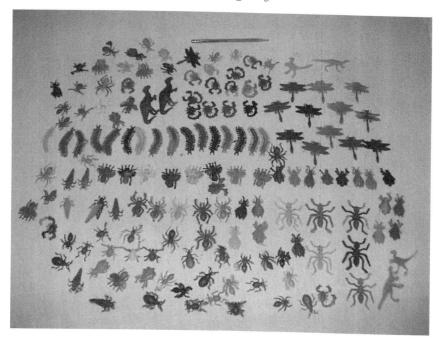

Andy's creepy crawler collection.

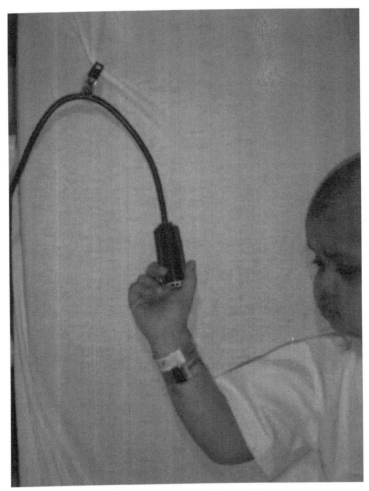

Andy's pain button for his morphine pump.

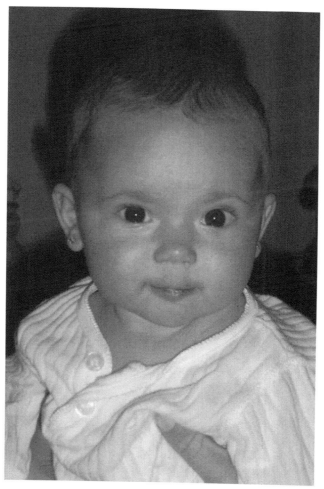

Sofia at home, waiting for Andy.

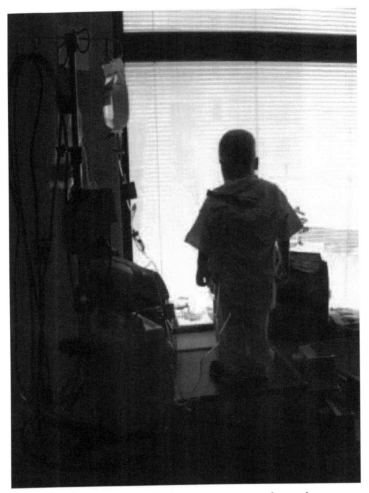

Andy watching the snow storm, on engraftment day.

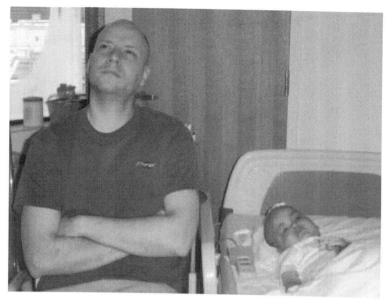

Andrés and Andy waiting.

Andy and nurse Kelli in the hallway of   6 West.

Andy's farewell T-shirts, decorated by his transplant nurses.

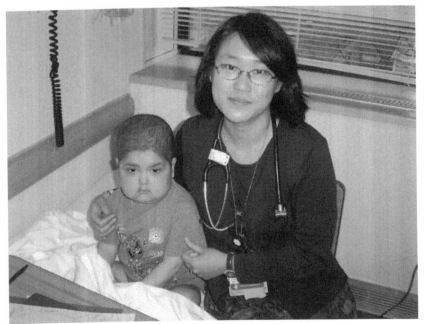

Andy on a checkup with Dr. Pai after discharge.

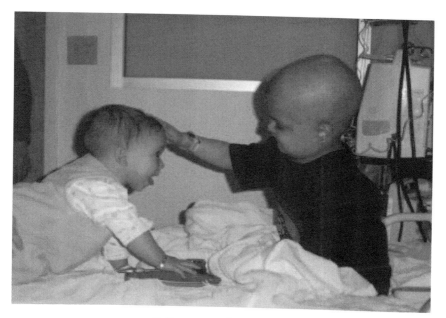

Sofía on a sneak visit to 6 West.

Sofía, Paulina, Andrés and Andy ready to go home.

Post-Transplant Life

Andy's road to recovery was neither straight nor smooth. In the next two years he suffered setbacks, re-hospitalizations and chronic colitis. We feared we'd never be able to free him from the prednisone that tamed his intestinal inflammation but still depressed his immunity. During one particularly bad colitis attack, Dr. Nurko even suggested he might be better off with a colostomy, the removal of his colon. We rejected that idea, opting to wait. In the meantime, Sofía's stem cells continued to re-educate Andy's immune system. His resistance to infection improved steadily. He was able to re-enter kindergarten—a high-output germ factory—in September, 2005, at age 6.

Two years after that, Andy's colitis had diminished so much we decided to take him off the steroids, despite Nurko's reluctance. Paulina's finely-honed intuition sensed that as long as we were vigilant about his diet and used our old friend Vancomycin as a preventive, Andy would be fine. Within weeks, his face changed dramatically. His photos from the first day of second grade show that his steroid "chipmunk cheeks" had disappeared and his high cheekbones—Paulina's—emerged. Paulina was right. He's been flare-up free since.

Paulina and I have no doubt that Andy's love for his sister was as therapeutic as anything. For him, Sofía's been a constant source of energy, affection, laughter and occasional fights. From the moment she took her first steps at 9 months, her *modus operandi* has been "anything you can do I can do better." She has pushed her brother hard to keep up. Because of her, Andy approaches life with more guts and gusto. He's still catching up to his peers in size, but approaches any challenge head-on. Today, in fifth grade, he's a soccer player, dancer (to Michael Jackson), explorer, movie buff, Boy Scout, lobster eater, reader and, best of all, a big brother.

Sofía, a first-grader, is a whirlwind of constant motion. She learned to swim at 5, and abandoned her bike's training wheels the same year. She loves all forms of physical activity, from trampoline-jumping to dancing to karate. She's a Justin Bieber fan, and loves to be the center of attention—the opposite of her brother.

Every summer Andy and Sofía spend a month in Mexico, visiting grandparents, aunts and uncles; playing and fighting with cousins; exploring the sights and speaking nonstop Spanish.

We've remained friends with Jordan and Katie Orange. A few years ago our two families took a Mexican vacation together while Jordan delivered a paper at an immunology conference in Merida. Dr. Orange has become an international expert on NEMO, with his own research lab at the University of Pennsylvania Medical School. He's still diagnosing children and helping their parents find treatment.

Andy still sees Dr. Pai for annual follow-up visits and she likes keeping tabs on our family, as does Dr. Geha. Dr. Nurko is still our gastroenterologist.

In 2006, Paulina and I realized we never wanted to be beyond a 45-minute drive to Children's Hospital. We decided to stay in the US permanently to raise our family. So we sold our condo in Mexico City and eventually bought a house in Boston's western suburbs. Sudbury's a town well-known for rural beauty and an excellent school system. Our house has a yard with a garden, swing set and trampoline. It's near woods and a pond, and on spring evenings Andy, Sofía and I like to catch frogs. We hold jumping competitions on the driveway before we let them go.

Paulina and I have pursued our personal goals, too. We've both keenly felt a desire to help other parents dealing with catastrophic illness, and to raise awareness and support for medical advances like the ones that saved our son. Paulina enrolled part-time in a local college and has been steadily completing courses in pediatric nursing. She hopes to work at Children's one day.

I worked for the family business for a while, setting up a satellite office in Boston, while also contributing to Children's Hospital's fundraising efforts as a motivational speaker. Eventually I became a full-time fundraiser in the hospital development office, the Children's Hospital Trust. I tell our story whenever I get the chance, especially if it helps put a human face on the issues of in vitro fertilization, pre-implantation genetic diagnosis and embryonic stem cell research.

Epilogue
Stem Cell Legacy

Four years after the transplant, with Andy and Sofía thriving, Paulina and I felt we could fulfill our dream of adding a third child to our family. This time, we didn't need a compatible genetic match; we just wanted another baby free of Andy's disease. Thanks once again to assisted fertility, we got 13 IVF embryos. The preimplantation genetic diagnosis test for NEMO showed only two of them were disease-free. Both were implanted in Paulina at Brigham & Women's Hospital in July 2008. But what of the other 11 embryos?

On implantation day, I called our old friend, Dr. Paul Lerou. Years ago as a neonatology resident, he'd spent time helping us understand Andy's ectodermal dysplasia diagnosis, the first clue to the NEMO mutation. He'd also been part of Andy's treatment team during many hospitalizations. I knew he was now working in the Stem Cell Program at Children's Hospital Boston, established in 2004, the year of Andy's transplant.

Headed by Director Leonard Zon, MD, and Associate Director George Daley, MD, PhD, the Stem Cell Program had become widely recognized as the world leader in blood stem cell research. It's one of the top programs worldwide perfecting techniques for using a patient's own cells to create replacements for damaged cells, thereby avoiding donor rejection issues.

Dr. Zon recently discovered a medication that amplifies blood stem cell formation three-fold. It's being developed as a way to produce abundant cells for stem cell transplants for immune systems which have been damaged by blood disease or chemotherapy. Dr. Daley, past president of the International Society for Stem Cell Research (ISSCR), is famous for many stem cell breakthroughs. Using animal models, he was the first researcher to transform embryonic stem cells into adult blood stem cells. The Daley lab, where Paul Lerou works, also is foremost in demonstrating that viable human stem cell lines can be derived from embryos and eggs that would ordinarily be discarded as medical waste.

When I told Lerou we wanted to donate the rest of our 5-day-old IVF embryos to his research he immediately grabbed an incubating canister and walked the two blocks from Children's to Brigham & Women's fertility clinic to retrieve them.

Eight weeks later, he invited me to his laboratory to see what had happened to those embryos.

His colleague, Akiko, had chemically treated the embryos—each a sac of about 200 cells—to remove the sac's clear outer membrane. This membrane would have helped them attach to a uterine wall, but once it was removed, they technically ceased being embryos and became simply masses of living stem cells. Using the equivalent of microscopic chopsticks, Akiko plated each cell mass on a nutrient-rich medium of feeder cells. Then the stem cells recovered for a few days in an incubator, untouched.

"It's always hard to wait without looking at them—it's like wanting to open the oven to check on a soufflé," Lerou said. "But they have to be undisturbed. You don't know if they'll successfully clump together and adhere to the feeder cells. Will they multiply? Or will they die? Akiko's really talented at this so our success rate is pretty good."

After he showed me the multiplying cells under the microscope, he continued, "After Akiko found outgrowth on two of the original cell masses, and these cells grew into a big enough colony, she dissected the mass into eight pieces, re-plating them on more feeder cells. Then each of these pieces grew into another colony of thousands—even millions—of cells. That's what you just looked at. We've now got two distinct, vigorous lines from your embryos, one female cell line *carrying* NEMO, and one male line which *has* the disease."

"What happens to them now?" I asked.

"These lines will join others with specific diseases in a bank we're developing. When we introduce certain chemicals to the cells, they'll start to develop into more specialized cells, the way they're already programmed to do. We already figured out the right chemicals to use that can prompt them to become blood cells. Then they're ready for us to study. We'll have a unique opportunity to investigate NEMO at its origins, when the immune system is being formed and there's a critical protein missing. Thanks to Jordan Orange and everyone else who contributed to Andy's diagnosis, we know precisely where the missing piece occurs. We'll look for all the ways this missing information and subsequent wayward development affects all the blood and immune components."

"Wow." I tried to grasp the significance. At the time of Andy's diagnosis, the idea of turning his potential death sentence into therapeutic gold would have been unfathomable. Now it was close to reality. The diseased cells Paulina and I had created would very possibly lead to better understanding, more effective therapies, even a complete cure for a fatal condition.

"We'll be sharing your cell lines with researchers all over the world," Lerou continued. "What you and your wife have given the Stem Cell Program—and Children's—is immensely valuable."

"It's no more valuable than what Children's Hospital gave us," I answered. "How could we not be willing to give anything we can to help other families going through what we did? You gave my son a future."

New Life

Meanwhile, our IVF luck was holding. On the day I brought our discarded embryos to Lerou's lab, Paulina was at Brigham & Women's Hospital, resting after the two disease-free embryos were implanted. One of them failed to attach, but the other signaled a resounding "Yes!" in a pregnancy test 10 days later. Our third child, a beautiful daughter we named Tania, was born in April, 2009. Today she's a happy, energetic toddler who wants only to follow after her sister and brother in everything they do.

We strive every day to be thankful, to be generous, to appreciate love and family, to live life as a precious gift. And we continue to be blessed.

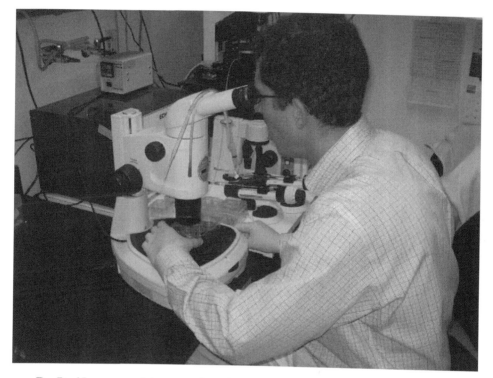

Dr. Paul Lerou examining our embryonic stem cell lines in his lab at Children's Hospital Boston.

Andy and Sofia, 2005

Articles in Medical Journals

Deficient natural killer cell cytotoxicity in patients with IKK-b/ NEMO mutations

Jordan S. Orange, et al.

J Clin Invest. 2002 June 1; 109(11): 1501–1509.

doi: 10.1172/JCI0214858.

PMCID: PMC150995

Finding NEMO: genetic disorders of NF-kB activation

Jordan S. Orange and Raif S. Geha

J Clin Invest. 2003 October 1; 112(7): 983–985.

Division of Immunology, Children's Hospital and Department of Pediatrics, Harvard Medical School, Boston, Massachusetts, USA

doi: 10.1172/JCI200319960.

PMCID: PMC200971

Characteristics of mycobacterial infection in patients with immunodeficiency and nuclear factore kB essential modulator mutation, with or without ectodermal dysplasia

Yang-Shia Dai, MD, et al.

Supported by Jeffrey Modell Foundation.

doi:10.1016/j.jaad.2004.05.03

Allogeneic transplantation successfully corrects immune defects, but not susceptibility to colitis, in a patient with nuclear factor-kappaB essential modulator deficiency.

Pai SY, et al.

J Allergy Clin Immunol. 2008 Dec; 122 (6):1113-1118.e1.

Epub 2008 Oct 11.

Locations - latitude and longitude

Hospital Angeles de las Lomas: 19.394463, -99.281806

Home Mexico: 19.406707,-99.261603

Hospital ABC: 19.400261,-99.203968

Kretschmer Office: 19.423545,-99.205918

Kretschmer Lab.: 19.409281,-99.154384

Children's Hospital Denver: 39.746297,-104.973481

National Jewish Hospital: 39.739211,-104.941868

Children's Hospital Boston: 42.337274,-71.10567

National Institutes of Health: 39.003286,-77.10454

Wayne State University: 42.355674,-83.068979

Microsort: 38.868511,-77.233137

Reproductive Genetics Institute: 41.933676,-87.648937

Fertility Center New England: 42.516667,-71.099213

Zonana Office: 45.497827,-122.685914

Thank you - Gracias

Gracias, Vero, por estar ahí con nosotros el día que nació Andy.

Dr. Maya, gracias por enseñarnos que algunos doctores simplemente están muy saturados.

Dr. Maulen, más o menos tenía razón, gracias. Gracias por enseñarnos que la gamma globulina no es cosa tan mala.

Dr. Kretschmer (rest in peace), thank you for saving his life on numerous occasions and for teaching me the most valuable lessons of my life. Thank you teaching me that "Absence of proof is not a proof of absence" and truisms.

Dr. Madrazo, gracias por tratar de entender esto.

Dr. Martínez-Natera, gracias porser el primero en mencionar indirectamente condiciones genéticas.

Enfermeras Hospital ABC, gracias por la introducción a bombas y catéteres (pudo haber estado peor...)

Dr. Sánchez gracias por sus cálculos y por enseñarnos que Andy podía recibir nutrición por las venas.

Dr. Gimenez, gracias por la introducción a la investigación médica básica.

Dr. Torres, gracias por haber estado ahí en Noche Buena y en Navidad en la sala de operaciones. Gracias por enseñarnos que tener un hoyo en el estómago (literalmente) no es tan malo.

Dr. Sokol, thank you for the introduction to gastroenterology.

Dr. Gelfand, thank you for teaching us that medical research comes in different languages.

Dr. Melgoza, gracias por ayudarnos a encontrar que los recursos de investigación médica en México no eran suficientes para ayudar a Andy. Gracias por recomendar salir de México.

Dr. Vazquez, gracias por cuidarlo, y gracias por cacharme cuando me desmayé.

Dr. Nurko, thank you for your trust and thank you for always being there when we need you. Thank you for having very good hands. Thank you for talking on the radio about Andy.

Dr. Turvey, thank you for the first written diagnosis and thank you for your help with official letters.

Joanna Hedstrom, thank you for your help with hospital bills.

Dr. Orange, thank you for your incredible mind. Thank you for your friendship. Thank you for discovering NEMO and thank you for the inspiration to create Andy's website. Thank you for inviting us for dinner and thank you for Andy's 2nd birthday party. Thank you for being there in the ER when I was away and saving his life. Thank you for letting us know that there's someone else out there. And thank you for teaching us that there's always an option.

Dr. Geha, thank you for knowing who we are and for being there all the time. Thank you for letting us step into your office any time and for answering emails so fast.

Nurse Ana Maria, thank you for teaching us how to take care of Andy.

Nurse Ruth, thank you for making us smile.

Nurse Aimee, thank you for teaching us that nurses also cry.

Dr. Gellis, thank you for helping us find about ectodermal dysplasia.

Thank you, Mary Kaye Richter, for answering our messages and referring us to Dr. Zonana.

7 East, thank you for being our second home and for the introduction to Boston. Thank you for teaching us how to do intramuscular injections.

Carole Ferguson, thank you for your friendship and for listening to us.

To parents of children who passed away while we were in the hospital, thank you for your spiritual influence. And to the children who passed away while we were in the hospital, rest in peace.

8 East, thank you for letting us paint the windows.

Dr. Borovoy, gracias por mantenerlo a salvo.

Mr. Mohammed, thank you for teaching me that being in the hospital with your child is tougher than being a prisoner of war.

Dr. Zonana, thank you for finding NEMO.

Dr. Murray, thank you for the introduction to genetic tests using a buccal swab.

Dr. Bale, thank you for confirming the genetic diagnosis.

Vicki and Fred Modell, thank you for telling us about transplants and thank you for all the invitations to the Red Sox games, dinner parties and boat trips. And thank you for all that you do for children with primary immune deficiencies.

Dr. Pai, thank you for being right. Thank you for following our story and for being right again.

Dr. Frank, thank you for talking to us about genetics.

Dr. Harris, thank you for telling me I could be a doctor.

Dr. Hughes, thank you for your generosity and your explanations about pre-implantation genetic diagnosis.

Laurie Strongin and Allen Goldberg, thank you for being PGD pioneers.

Dianne Gates, thank you for all the in vitro fertilization medication vials.

Dr. Jain, thank you for knowing so much about NEMO.

Dr. Cardone, thank you for giving us more options.

Dr. Hardy, thank you for implanting the right cells and advising us to let them settle.

Max Leonardo, gracias por las medicinas de fertilización in vitro. Y Lupita gracias por tu ayuda.

Renee Genovese, thank you for being so professional when talking about genetics.

Arden Hill, thank you for teaching us that playing with food is not a bad thing.

Vicki Nahmad, thank you for introducing us to the school system in Massachusetts.

Shannon Hennig, Holly Suda, Leigh-Anne Porter, Laura Merl, Kim Deveau Dern, thank you for teaching Andy how to eat.

Elyse Topp-Poirier, thank you for running the Boston marathon for Andy twice.

Brian Serroul, thank you for running the Boston marathon for Andy.

Dr. Samuels, thank you for teaching us about regular pediatrics.

Jorge Luis d'Argence, gracias por correr el maratón de Paris por Andy.

Dr. Verlinsky, thank you for your generosity and for doing what you do.

Dr. Butte, thank you for your friendship and for keeping us in touch with other families with primary immune deficiencies.

Dr. Lemon, thank you for saving his life.

Nurse Kelli, thank you for your friendship, thank you for making it fun and doing it right. Thank you for defying gravity and for putting a smile on Andy's face. Thank you for running the marathon for Andy.

Dr. Sachs, thank you for treating us like normal people and thank you for reading all those emails.

Dr. Lehman, thank you for saving Andy's life and thank you for taking care of Sofía. Thank you for making it easier.

Nurse Maura, thank you for arriving just in time and for saving Andy's life.

Nurse Lissa, thank you for talking to me about gadgets in the middle of the night.

Dr. Callaway, thank you for making it fun, your political career is not over.

Nurse Robin, thank you for directing the World Series trophy to Andy's room.

Nurse Lissa P., thank you for teaching us that nurses also use skateboards.

Six West, thank you for showing us the fun part of tough things and difficult moments.

To the phlebotomists, thank you for trying your best.

To helpful people we've never met directly, like lab technicians and pharmacists, thank you.

Thank you Matt Cyr for writing about Little Sister Big Gift.

Thank you Bess for following our story.

To Andy's blood donors:

A los donadores de sangre:

- Mauricio Hernández, gracias, tienes muy buenas venas.

- Jorge Elliot, gracias.

- Ana Jose Z. de Gonzalez, gracias.

- Children's Hospital Denver blood bank, thank you.

- Salvador Albino, gracias.

- Agustin Hernández Aguirre, gracias.
- Children's Hospital Boston blood bank, thank you.

To the more than 100 people who registered (or at least tried to register) as stem cell donors through a public registry for Andy, thank you.

A las más de 100 personas que se registraron (o por lo menos trataron de registrarse) como donadores de células madre por medio de un registro público por Andy, gracias.

And to the more than 80 people who registered through our own registry (via FedEx) and donated $80 to do it, thank you.

Y a las más de 80 personas que se registraron por medio de nuestro propio registro (vía FedEx) y donaron $800 para hacerlo, gracias.

A las voluntarias que cuidaron a Andy, Claudia, Ivonne, Carolina, Ana Jose, Myrna, Rocio, Male, Ana Jose Rosas, Dolores (Lita), Mariana, Rosa Elena y Alejandra, gracias.

Thank you to Andy's teachers at Lawrence School, and NorthEastern, Burr, Nixon and Loring Schools.

Thank you, Roberta, for being Andy's tutor and for your friendship.

Thank you, Mala Shah, for your help.

Thank you to our family members and friends who followed the story. Thank you for the messages of support and for your prayers.

Gracias a nuestros familiares y amigos que siguieron la historia, gracias por los mensajes de apoyo y por sus oraciones.

A mi Papá, mi Suegro and my Abuelo gracias por su apoyo financiero.

Opapa, thank you for calling so often to see how we were doing. Thank you for visiting us.

To those of you who have a "I helped Andy" T-shirt, baseball cap, or flash light key chain, thank you. Thanks for buying raffle tickets, bracelets, calling cards, golf balls, a bag of coffee or a box of peaches.   And thank you to the sponsors of all the products.

A las personas que tengan una camiseta "Yo ayude a Andy", gorra, lámpara, llavero, gracias. O a quienes compraron boletos de la rifa, pulseras, tarjetas telefónicas, pelotas de golf, bolsas de café, o una caja de duraznos, gracias. Y a los patrocinadores de esos productos, gracias.

To the people who didn't buy anything but did send a donation, thank you.

A las personas que no compraron algo pero si mandaron un donativo, gracias.

Special thanks to the person who bought a door through Andy's website (yes, we sold a door through Andy's website).

Thank you, Ricardo, for all the autographs. And thank you to all the people who helped us find autographs.

Gracias, Doña Margot, por su apoyo y por organizar la fiesta de cumpleaños de Andy en Tuxtla.

Gracias, Doña Soco, por sus oraciones y por tener el cirio prendido.

Gracias, Victor, por tu ayuda vendiendo boletos de la rifa y a todos los demás voluntarios que vendieron un total de novecientosnoventa y nueve boletos. Nat, Pericles, Diego Ch., Ale d'A., Francisco Gonzalez, Antonio Mayer, Paty Piña, Ana Paula O., Maaike del Villar, David Castillo, Chendo V., Mimi Gómez, Male F., Fernando B., Maguis, Luz Ma. d'A., Alma Rosa, José Manuel O., Lucia F., Jerry Galván, Marysela R.,Eugenio S., Ileana, Kike, gracias.

Gracias a Victor por hablar sobre Andy frente a cientos de personas.

Gracias, Carmina y Manolo, por enseñarnos sobre transplantes.

Thank you to the 6 West parent who found one of our post-it clues hidden behind a mirror, instructing Kelli to go to www.andy.org.mx for the next clue.

Gracias, Victor, por hablar sobre Andy en la radio. Y gracias por las ideas para reunir fondos.

Gracias, Maguis y Ana Jose, por vender tarjetas telefónicas y a todas los voluntarios que vendieron tarjetas telefónicas. Y gracias a las personas que compraron las tarjetas telefónicas e hicieron llamadas.

Thank you to all the people who left a message at Andy's website.

Gracias a todas las personas que dejaron un mensaje en la página de Andy.

Thank you, Mark Porter, for running the Boston marathon for Andy.

Gracias, Victor, por correr el maratón de Boston por Andy.

Thank you, Tim McQuade, for running the Boston marathon for Andy.

Gracias, Don Alfredo y Lupita, por su apoyo. Y gracias, Lupita, por el discurso tan bonito durante el bautizo de Sofía.

Gracias, Papá, por hablar acerca de Andy frente a cientos de personas. Gracias por el apoyo espiritual. Gracias por llorar conmigo. Y gracias por tu carta.

Gracias, Mamá, por leer este libro antes que nadie y gracias por hablar sobre Andy en el radio. Gracias por ser tan positiva. Te extraño mucho.

Thank you, Sofía, for donating your cells. Thank you, Andy, for helping us find Sofía.

Happiness is meant to be shared.

Made in the USA
Lexington, KY
17 November 2011